TRAMPING IN NEW ZEALAND
40 GREAT TRAMPING TRIPS

For the hard-working Department of Conservation staff
who maintain tracks and huts throughout the country,
and also the volunteers from tramping and hunting clubs who do the same.

TRAMPING IN NEW ZEALAND
40 GREAT TRAMPING TRIPS

Shaun Barnett
Maps by Geographx

 potton & burton

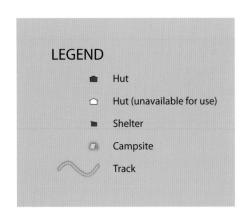

LEGEND

🏠 Hut

⌂ Hut (unavailable for use)

◼ Shelter

⛺ Campsite

〜 Track

First published in 2006 by Craig Potton Publishing

Reprinted 2007, 2008, 2010, 2012

Fully revised in 2015 by Potton & Burton
98 Vickerman Street, PO Box 5128, Nelson, New Zealand
www.pottonandburton.co.nz

© Maps by Geographx

© Photography and text: Shaun Barnett and individual photographers

ISBN 978 1 927213 72 8

Printed in China by Midas Printing International Ltd

ACKNOWLEDGEMENTS

Grateful thanks to my family, Tania, Tom, Lee and Lexi, who either came on trips, or put up with my absence on many other tramps.

I'd also like to thank a number of people who have been fine companions in the hills: Daryl Ball, David Barnes, Angela Barnett, Grant Barnett, Rob Brown, Dave Chowdhury, Andy Dennis, Tony Gates, Dave Hansford, Susan Harper, Debbie Hager, Nicky Hager, Marley Kuys, Saskia Kuys, Andrew Lynch, Ken MacIver, Chris Maclean, Geoff Norman, Darryn Pegram, Jock Phillips, Bruce Postill, Andy Reisinger, Derek Shaw, Geoff Spearpoint, Oliver Snow and Mark Stanton.

I am also grateful to the Department of Conservation (DOC) staff who helped check draft chapters in the first edition.

The DOC website (www.doc.govt.nz) has excellent information about all of the tracks in this book, and readers are advised to check it for any updates or hazard warnings before embarking on their trip. It goes without saying that any mistakes are mine alone; if you find a significant error, email (info@pottonandburton.co.nz) or write to the publisher, as I'd appreciate knowing about it for future editions.

Unless otherwise credited, all photographs were taken by Shaun Barnett/Black Robin Photography.

Edelweiss, Polar Range, Arthur's Pass National Park

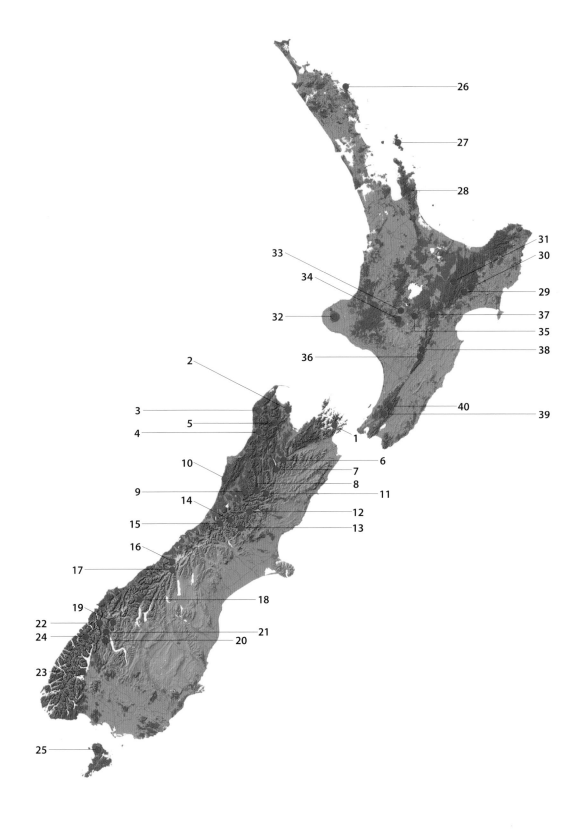

CONTENTS

INTRODUCTION

… to write a guide book is to poke out a neck as scapegoat… On your head will fall the imprecations of parties who wander in circles because they did not find the entrance of the track you so concisely described. Your directions were dehydrated, as it were, and those who came after did not reconstitute your stew with care. So be willing to take blame and to lose tail feathers. It will be natural for any unfortunates coming down the wrong bank of a river or the difficult side of an icefall to curse the absent chronicler. Do they lose an hour in the scrub or skin on the ridge, find impasse on the glacier or defeat on the skyline, mislay a hut in the dark or a toothbrush in the mist, it will be on your careless summary so fluently compiled.

John Pascoe, *The Southern Alps: from the Kaikoura to the Rangitata* (1956)

Tramping is a well-established New Zealand tradition, with a history dating back more than a century. Known in other countries as hiking, bush walking or trekking, tramping is a uniquely New Zealand term, and one fitting the style of walking encountered here – often rough, frequently wet, but regularly inspiring.

New Zealand is arguably the best country in the world in which to tramp. Very few other countries offer such a diversity of terrain, ranging from coastal to mountain, in such a small area. New Zealand has tracks in areas that feature active volcanoes, hot springs, moss-laden rainforests, ragged fault ranges, glacier-carved valleys, island-studded lakes and golden-sand coastlines.

Because New Zealand has been isolated from other landmasses for more than 65 million years, much of the flora and fauna here is also unique. Among many other examples, creatures like the kea (the only alpine parrot in the world) and plants like the cabbage tree (the world's tallest lily) help make the experience of tramping here distinctive.

Furthermore, the network of tracks and huts maintained by the Department of Conservation (DOC) is rarely bettered anywhere else. Only a few countries, such as Norway and Italy, have anything like the number of backcountry huts that New Zealand offers. Unlike many European nations, however, most New Zealand huts are largely self-catering,

and trampers need to be fully self-reliant for food, cookers, sleeping bags and equipment – so preserving something of pioneer traditions. There are a few exceptions: on the Milford, Routeburn, Hollyford and Greenstone–Caples tracks, private companies offer a catered, guided option using private huts. However, only the independent alternatives are described in this book.

Tramps selected for this book were chosen from throughout New Zealand, reflecting a range of length, difficulty, terrain and natural history. However, most were chosen with the novice or casual tramper in mind; few of the tramps featured are beyond the abilities of a moderately fit person with modest experience. None involves any serious off-track travel, and generally the standard of huts and tracks is high. An exception is the North West Circuit on Stewart Island/Rakiura; this long tramp is demanding not only because of the need to carry food for 10–12 days, but also because of the frequently muddy sections of track.

Selecting what I consider to be the crème de la crème of the country's easier tramps was necessarily subjective. In choosing, I tried to keep in mind a range of tramping trips in different types of terrain, and also attempted to get a basic nationwide coverage. Although someone else might argue for an entirely different list, together the 40 tramps detailed here do reflect the great diversity of New Zealand tramping.

Trampers, Copland Valley, Westland Tai Poutini National Park

Great Walks

New Zealand has eight 'Great Walks' (and one 'Great Paddle', the Whanganui Journey, which is a trip for kayakers, not trampers). These are considered New Zealand's premier tracks, and most have become internationally renowned – notably the Milford Track, which has long carried the byline 'the finest walk in the world'. All Great Walks have a level of facilities that is of a higher standard than on most other New Zealand tramping tracks. Due to their popularity, both with New Zealanders and overseas visitors, all the Great Walks have a booking system in place for huts and campsites (tel: 0800 NZ GREAT WALKS (0800 694 732), website: www.greatwalks.co.nz, email: greatwalks@doc.govt.nz).

This book details seven of the eight Great Walks, including the Lake Waikaremoana, Tongariro Northern Circuit, Abel Tasman, Heaphy, Routeburn, Milford and Kepler tracks. The Rakiura Track on Stewart Island/Rakiura was excluded because it overlaps with the North West Circuit.

Length and difficulty

Each tramp is classified according to difficulty: 'easy', 'medium' or 'hard', with some in between. By far the majority fall into the easy and medium categories.

wHowever, the level of difficulty does depends very much on the season and weather conditions. Wet weather could very well turn a medium tramp into a hard, or even impossible one, while winter snow may transform a medium trip into one that requires mountaineering skills. When selecting a tramp it is also important to take the abilities of all party members into consideration.

Easy Expect gentle terrain, well-marked tracks, few if any river crossings, and walking times of 4–5 hours per day, or less.

Medium Trampers may come across unbridged river crossings, steep sections of track, or some travel on open tops. Travel times could be 5–7 hours per day.

Hard These trips will often entail walking for up to 7–8 hours per day, and will often require some navigation skills.

The length of each section of the tramps is also given in kilometres, but this is usually a less reliable indicator of the effort required than the time. On a good surface, such as that found on most Great Walks, a fit tramper may cover 4–6 kph. However, on a rough track, travel is usually more like 2 kph, and sometimes slower, depending on conditions. The degree of ascent and descent naturally affects your speed as well – as a good rule of thumb, expect to cover about 300 m of ascent per hour.

Te Araroa – New Zealand's Trail

This long-distance trail runs the length of New Zealand, from Cape Reinga in the north, to Bluff at the bottom of the South Island. Officially opened in 2011, the 3000 km trail is New Zealand's equivalent of the Appalachian or Pacific Crest trails in the USA, the Bibbulmun Track in Australia, or the Pennine Way in Britain.

Te Araroa follows the route of several tracks in this book, including the Queen Charlotte and Harper Pass tracks, and parts of the Travers–Sabine Circuit, St James Walkway and Cass–Lagoon Saddle Track (see www.teararoa.org.nz).

Keeping information up to date

Although every effort has been made to ensure information in this guide is both correct and up to date, please remember that wild places change constantly. Floods alter rivers, volcanoes erupt from time to time, and storms or earthquakes can devastate forests and tracks. Careless fires do, surprisingly frequently, reduce huts to ashes. Furthermore, the condition of tracks and huts varies according to how recently they have been maintained. For these reasons, trampers should always check with the local DOC visitor centre for updates before their intended trip. The relevant DOC telephone number has been given for each tramp. DOC's website (www.doc.govt.nz) is also an excellent source of information, including downloadable brochures for many tracks.

If you do find any safety hazards – such as a bridge washed out, or a new slip on a track – please report it to DOC through their emergency hotline (tel: 0800 DOC HOT (0800 362 468)).

Maps

The maps in this book are digital images created by Roger Smith, the director of Geographx, a Wellington-based company that specialises in advanced digital mapping. Roger's superb maps – perhaps 'oblique panorama' is a better description – do what no photograph can achieve: they offer a complete overview of each tramp, showing tracks, huts and major features. For more information, refer to *Landforms: The shaping of New Zealand*, in the Further Reading section (see page 142).

While these maps indicate tracks, huts and major topographical features, they are not intended to be used for navigation – for this you should purchase a Land Information New Zealand Topo50 series 1:50,000 scale topographical map or appropriate track map. The correct map(s) number for each tramp (e.g. Topo50 BP29 Endeavour Inlet) is included in the fact file at the end of each chapter.

Note that true left refers to the left bank of a river when facing downstream, and true right to the right bank.

Seasons and weather

New Zealand's temperate latitude fools some visitors to this country into thinking that the weather will always be mild. Although tempered by its maritime surrounds, New Zealand's position in the path of the Roaring Forties and its mountainous terrain combine to produce some of the most changeable and unpredictable meteorological conditions on the planet. In the mountains, where most of the tramps in this book are located, snow can fall at any time of year, although obviously it is rarer during summer. Some parts of New Zealand, particularly the West Coast and Fiordland, experience some of the highest rainfall in the world – some 7000–9000 mm of rain falls at Milford Sound annually, while in 1998 a West Coast valley near Hokitika received more than 15 m of rain! Heavy rain can make sections of some tracks impassable and rivers unfordable in as little as a few hours.

Trampers need to plan around the weather. Always obtain a forecast before you leave, and be prepared to pare back or change your plans accordingly. If river levels do rise overnight, be prepared to wait another night at the hut or camp. Once the rain stops, river levels will usually fall as fast as they rose.

As a general rule, late summer and autumn (January to April) are the best seasons for tramping in New Zealand. During these times the temperatures are at their mildest, the rainfall is generally less and the probability of snow is unlikely. Spring and early summer (September to December) offer the delights of alpine flowers, but in mountainous terrain avalanches may pose a risk. For those who are suitably equipped and experienced, winter (May to August) offers its own rewards: generally fewer people, sometimes crisp, long spells of fine weather, and all the glories of snow-capped mountains.

Taking into account the amount of daylight is also important when planning your tramp. For example, in midsummer Stewart Island/Rakiura experiences 16 hours of daylight, but by midwinter this is reduced to as little as eight hours. In more northerly latitudes the difference is not as extreme, but even in Northland you can expect only 10 hours of daylight around the winter solstice.

For further information, check out www.metservice.co.nz and www.avalanche.net.nz.

Huts and hut fees

New Zealand's hut network – which includes more than 1000 backcountry huts – is unique in the world, but requires your support if it is to be maintained. By far the majority of huts are owned and managed by DOC, although a significant number are maintained by tramping, hunting and alpine clubs.

DOC charges modest hut fees for staying overnight in most huts, excepting very small huts or bivs, which are free. Hut fees by no means cover the cost of maintaining all New Zealand's tracks and huts, let alone replacing those that are occasionally destroyed by fires or fall down from old age. But by paying hut fees, you are doing your bit to enable future generations – New Zealanders and overseas visitors alike – to enjoy the backcountry.

Charges vary according to the hut and its facilities, rated

Sunset from Mt Heale Hut, Great Barrier Island

by DOC in the following categories: serviced ($15/night), standard ($5/night) and basic/bivvy (free). Serviced huts, like those on the Wangapeka, Greenstone and Hollyford tracks, cost $15/night, are likely to have an indoor sink and running water, and usually have heating and sometimes cooking facilities. Standard huts, such as Makino Hut in the Kaweka Range, usually just have mattresses and perhaps a woodburner or open fire. A basic shelter, like the Flora Valley rock shelters, have mattresses but not much else.

Great Walks and alpine huts have a different fee structure, which usually varies according to the season. Excepting those huts on the Abel Tasman Coastal, Te Urewera and Rakiura tracks, all Great Walks huts have gas cooking facilities and cost between $22/night and $54/night during the peak summer season. For all other huts, you will need to carry your own cooking stove and fuel.

Hut tickets can be purchased from most DOC offices and information centres, and Great Walks hut bookings can be made online at www.doc.govt.nz. Youths aged under 18 are free on Great Walks huts but must still book. Children aged under 11 are free at all huts.

For those doing a lot of tramping (say spending more than 20 nights in a backcountry hut during a year), a good-value option is to purchase a Backcountry Hut Pass. These cost $122 for adults and $61 for youths (aged 11–17) for an annual pass, or $92 for adults and $46 for youths for a six-month pass. They enable use of all huts except Great Walks huts, and Mueller, Welcome Flat and Pinnacles huts. A 30 per cent discount on the annual pass fee is available for members of Federated Mountain Clubs of New Zealand, the New Zealand Mountain Safety Council and the New Zealand Deerstalkers' Association.

Most huts have logbooks for visitors to record their intentions and impressions. These not only provide a record for search and rescue purposes, but also often contain amusing anecdotes or interesting information on alternative routes.

Hut etiquette

At night or during bad weather, the hut forms the focus of the tramping experience, something that is part of New Zealand's backcountry tradition. A few simple courtesies help make the experience an enjoyable one for all, even in a crowded hut.

Always make room for newcomers, even if the hut is nearing capacity. When the hut is full, consider using a tent if you have one. Inside, keep your gear tidy and contained, and try not to spread out too much. Remove wet boots before entering the hut to keep the floor clean and dry. Cook with ventilation, conserve firewood, and don't overheat the hut to the discomfort of others. When leaving, make sure all benches and tables are clean, sweep the floor, close all windows and doors, and ensure you've replaced any firewood used. If you have spare room in your rubbish bag, consider taking out any leftover detritus – it's surprising how quickly huts can fill with 'forgotten' waste.

You can't go too wrong if you follow the rule, 'Leave the hut as you would hope to find it.'

Water and conservation

The New Zealand backcountry is blessed with some of the cleanest water on the planet. Care needs to be taken when camping or toileting to ensure it stays that way.

Do not use soap or detergent in lakes or streams, and where possible use toilets. If there is no long drop, go to the toilet at least 100 m away from water sources, and bury your waste in a shallow 'cat scrape'. When camping, take care not to pitch your tent in a fragile area, and refrain from hacking poles out of saplings.

While the waterborne parasite giardia is present in some backcountry waterways, there are still significant areas where you can safely drink straight from the stream. If in doubt, carry water treatments, boil the water for five minutes or use a water filter.

Have consideration for the environment; don't take anything natural, and don't leave anything unnatural. Carry out all your rubbish and any you find. Avoid lighting fires when they are unnecessary (in summer) or during a fire ban. When fires are necessary, keep them small and, where fireplaces exist, use them. Dismantle outdoor fireplaces after use.

Safety and equipment

There is not the scope in this book to give a detailed description of equipment and safety, but a brief list of what should be carried for a typical tramp is as follows: sleeping bag, billy, burner, fuel, warm woolly hat, sunhat, gloves, raincoat, warm jersey or fleece, two pairs of polypropylene or woollen long johns, two wool or polypropylene tops, a pair of shorts, first-aid kit, mug, plate, utensils, two pairs of warm socks, maps, compass, sunscreen, candles, matches, and enough food for the trip duration plus a few extra snacks and one extra meal. For some trips you may need to take a tent, or at least a flysheet and sleeping mat. In winter you may need to add an ice axe, crampons, sunglasses, more warm gear, extra fuel and extra food. Trampers should consider carrying a PLB (personal locator beacon), also known as an EPIRB, which can be used to alert authorities in the event of an accident or emergency. Many clubs and outdoor stores hire these out at modest rates. *The New Zealand Tramper's Handbook* by Sarah Bennett and Lee Slater provides an excellent introduction to tramping, and the Federated Mountain Clubs' *Safety in the Mountains* by Robin McNeill offers sound advice on tramping skills.

You should leave your intentions, including possible bad weather alternatives, with a trusted friend who can, in the event of your party becoming overdue, be relied upon to contact the police and Land Search and Rescue (LandSAR). During your tramp you should also fill in hut books, even if you do not stay in the hut, so that your route can be followed in the event that you become overdue or have an accident.

Remember that rivers are the biggest hazard in the backcountry and cause the most deaths. You should be well versed in the current New Zealand Mountain Safety Council river-crossing techniques, and have practised these before needing to use them in a real situation. Many tramping clubs offer introductory courses on river crossing, bushcraft and navigation. The website of the Federated Mountain Clubs of New Zealand (www.fmc.org.nz) has a list of affiliated tramping and alpine clubs.

The New Zealand Mountain Safety Council also has many good brochures and manuals on safety in the outdoors (see www.mountainsafety.org.nz).

Safety with wildlife

Few animals in New Zealand pose much threat to trampers. The country has no snakes or large carnivorous mammals, and only one poisonous spider – the very rare katipo, which lives only in coastal areas. Introduced pigs and deer will normally try to avoid you, but can be dangerous if threatened. The main hunting season for deer is during March and April, and in these months trampers should be aware of the presence of hunters.

Introduced wasps are a significant hazard, particularly during summer and autumn. Wasps have reached plague proportions in parts of the backcountry, notably in the parks around Nelson and the upper West Coast. Trampers should carry antihistamine cream and tablets, and wear gaiters to minimise the risk of stings. Those who are highly allergic to wasp stings should probably avoid Nelson's national parks between December and May.

On the coastal section of tracks like the Hollyford or North West Circuit, you may encounter New Zealand fur

Forest, Ruapani Track, Te Urewera

seals. It is best to observe these marine mammals from a respectful distance, and do not get between them and their escape route into the sea. Bull seals can be aggressive during the mating season, as can females when they have pups.

Two native birds, the alpine parrot, or kea, and the woodhen, or weka, often delight trampers with their antics, but both will thieve gear if given an opportunity. Kea may even destroy unattended tents, and are particularly mischievous in areas like Cascade Saddle and Arthur's Pass. Please refrain from feeding kea or weka; human foods are bad for their health, and encourage them into more trouble!

Finally, happy tramping. May the weather god Huey smile benevolently during your trip!

QUEEN CHARLOTTE TRACK
MARLBOROUGH SOUNDS 4–5 DAYS

During his three journeys to New Zealand in the eighteenth century, Captain James Cook spent more time in the Marlborough Sounds than anywhere else. It's not hard to see why: the relatively benign climate, the sheltered, intricate coastline and the lush coastal forest all combine to create a landscape not replicated elsewhere in New Zealand.

While farming and forestry have significantly altered the landscapes since Cook's time, much of the area remains forested and in a natural or regenerating state.

Tracks have long existed throughout the Marlborough Sounds, but it was not until DOC ranger Roy Grose began to negotiate access across private land to connect trails in a series of DOC reserves along the Queen Charlotte Sound that the existing Queen Charlotte Track became a reality. In recent years, the 71 km track, which connects Ship Cove (Meretoto) with Anakiwa, has become increasingly popular. Aside from the coastal scenery, the main attraction of the track is the diversity of accommodation en route, which ranges from the six basic DOC campsites to luxury bed and breakfasts.

Well defined and well marked, the track should not present any problems to trampers of modest fitness. While the entire route normally takes between three and five days, road access and water-taxi transport make a whole range of shorter options possible. Upon request, water-taxi operators can also transport packs for trampers.

Trampers must purchase a Queen Charlotte Track Land Cooperative Pass ($18 per person for five days, or $25 for an annual pass), which contributes to the upkeep of those sections of the track that cross private land (see www.qctlc.com). Passes can be purchased at local i-SITEs, a dispensing machine at Anakiwa and some businesses near the track. Visitors should respect the areas of private land by staying on the track, thereby ensuring the continued willingness of landowners to allow public access. Trampers should expect to meet mountain bikers, except between 1 December and 28 February, when bikes are not allowed on the Ship Cove to Kenepuru Saddle section.

Ship Cove (Meretoto) to Resolution Bay
2 hours, 4.5 km

Water-taxi transport to Ship Cove (Meretoto) is needed to access the start of the track. Ship Cove (Meretoto) became Captain Cook's home away from home during his New Zealand voyages. Here he made repairs to his ships, rested the crew, and replenished supplies of water and food. Altogether, he and his crews spent some 100 days here. The area surrounding the cove is now a historic reserve, with a memorial to Cook, information panels and a shelter (camping is not permitted at the cove).

Many walkers choose to divert first up a side-track that leads to an attractive waterfall (30 minutes return). From Ship Cove (Meretoto) the Queen Charlotte Track climbs 230 m through forest onto a ridge, where there is an excellent viewpoint overlooking the outer Queen Charlotte Sound and the distant North Island on one side, and the Kaikoura Range on the other. Beyond, the track descends to reach Resolution Bay (named after one of Cook's ships), where the first of the DOC campsites on the track is located at Schoolhouse Bay.

Sunrise, Bay of Many Coves

Resolution Bay to Camp Bay, Endeavour Inlet
6–8 hours, 22 km

From Resolution Bay the Queen Charlotte Track skirts the shore, then begins a climb over Tawa Saddle, eventually curling round into Endeavour Inlet – named after another of Cook's ships. The track gradually descends towards the shoreline, passing Furneaux Lodge, where cabin and backpacker accommodation is available. Nearby, a side-track leads to another waterfall.

From the head of Endeavour Inlet, it's possible to undertake a two-hour side-trip up the Antimony Mines Track to sites where this ore (used in pewter, solder, ammunition and batteries) was mined between 1873 and 1901.

After crossing the head of Endeavour Inlet, the Queen Charlotte Track sidles around another headland to reach Big Bay, then Camp Bay, where the second of the DOC campsites is located. Nearby Punga Cove offers more options for accommodation, and there is also the privately operated Miners Camp and Madsen's Camp.

Camp Bay to Torea Saddle and Cowshed Bay
8–10 hours, 23 km

This is the hardest section of the track, along which it is usually necessary to carry water. From Camp Bay the track climbs up to Kenepuru Saddle, where the first views of Kenepuru Sound open out. The track then largely follows the crest of the ridge separating Kenepuru Sound from Queen Charlotte Sound, offering fine panoramas, and several times reaching as high as 400 m above sea-level. DOC campsites exist above the Bay of Many Coves and at Black Rock Camp, above Kumutoto Bay. Those wanting more up-market accommodation can find it at Bay of Many Coves Resort,

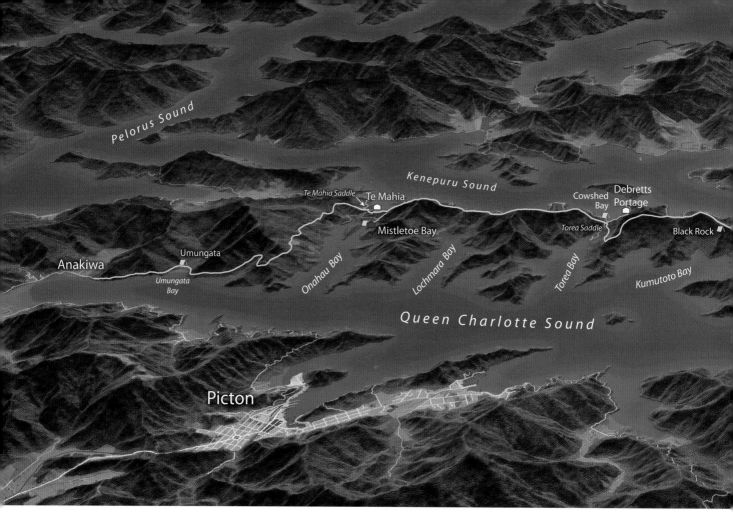

accessible on a side-track at the Bay of Many Coves.

The Queen Charlotte Track remains on the ridge as far as Torea Saddle, the narrow point between Torea and Portage bays. Here, the track intersects Torea Road, which is followed down to the shoreline at Portage Bay. Nearby, the Portage Hotel and Debretts offer accommodation, or alternatively there is the DOC campsite at Cowshed Bay.

Torea Saddle to Te Mahia Saddle and Mistletoe Bay 3–4 hours, 8 km

Back at Torea Saddle, the main track continues westwards, again on the ridge crest. The forest here is still regenerating from earlier fires, with manuka and gorse predominating.

Near Te Mahia Saddle, the track intersects a road that descends to Mistletoe Bay, where there are cabins and a campsite managed by the Mistletoe Bay Trust. There is alternative accommodation at Te Mahia Bay (on Kenepuru Sound on the other side of the saddle).

Te Mahia Saddle to Anakiwa 3–4 hours, 8 km

Back at Te Mahia Saddle, the main track follows the Mistletoe Bay road for a short distance, before diverting from it. The track climbs through mature forest – some of the loveliest on the entire route – before beginning a gentle descent back down to the shore at Umungata Bay, where the last of the DOC campsites is situated. Beyond, the track largely hugs the forested shoreline, ending at the Anakiwa Outward Bound School.

Grade Easy

Maps Topo50 BP29 Endeavour Inlet, BQ28 Havelock, BQ29 Waikawa

Access The Queen Charlotte Track can be accessed by road or boat from Picton. Road access points include: Anakiwa, Mistletoe Bay/Te Mahia Saddle, Torea Saddle and Kenepuru Saddle. Boat access includes: Anakiwa, Waterfall Bay, Mistletoe Bay, Torea Bay, Camp Bay, Endeavour Inlet, Resolution Bay and Ship Cove.

Campsites The six self-register DOC campsites on the track are located at: Schoolhouse Bay (6 tent sites), Camp Bay (20 tent sites), Bay of Many Coves (6 tent sites), Black Rock (4 tent sites), Cowshed Bay (30 tent sites) and Umungata Bay (25 tent sites). Carry cash to pay camp fees on site. Another campsite at Mistletoe Bay (20 sites) is managed by a trust.

Note Please respect private property through which the track passes. Sections of the track crossing private land may be closed at times. During extreme fire risk, the whole track may be closed.

Information and booking DOC, Picton i-SITE, The Foreshore, Picton, tel: 03 520 3113, email: picton@i-site.org.nz

ABEL TASMAN COAST TRACK
ABEL TASMAN NATIONAL PARK 3–5 DAYS

Outstanding coastal scenery dominates this track, one of New Zealand's eight Great Walks and the most popular in the country. Beginning in Golden Bay and ending at Marahau, the 60 km track takes a leisurely four to five days, but shorter sections can easily be planned using water-taxi transport.

When it became New Zealand's fourth national park in 1942, Abel Tasman was a milestone in many ways. All three of New Zealand's previous national parks centred on inland mountainous areas. Not only was Abel Tasman a coastal park, but many areas of the original forest had earlier been cleared and were regenerating. Creating a national park in an area that was not pristine was another first for the country. Its realisation was largely due to the dedicated efforts of conservationist Perrine Moncrieff, who foresaw the need to protect coastal areas and prevent further destruction of the forest.

Golden-sand beaches, granite headlands and lush forests all feature on the walk. Several large huts are spaced along the track at regular intervals, and many other bays offer delightful campsites. Abel Tasman's beaches are awash with people for most of the year, and even in winter don't expect solitude. However, the compensation is delightful coastal walking, year-round.

Walkers should note that some inlets on the track cannot be crossed at high tide, and must plan their trip around the low tide accordingly.

Wainui Inlet to Whariwharangi Hut (19 bunks)
2 hours, 5.7 km

Maori carvings mark the start to the Abel Tasman Coastal Track, a reminder that the first encounter between Europeans and Maori occurred near here in 1642 when Dutch seafarer Abel Tasman arrived in Golden Bay. After following the estuary around Wainui Inlet for a few hundred metres, the gorse-fringed track climbs to a saddle (at 180 m the highest point on the track) overlooking Whariwharangi Bay. From the saddle, the track descends beside a stream to emerge at the hut and campsite, set back from the beach. The hut, originally built in 1897, is a historic homestead dating from the area's farming past.

Whariwharangi Hut to Totaranui
3–3.5 hours, 9.8 km

From Whariwharangi Hut, follow the track down to the beach, then head right until track markers indicate where to re-enter the forest. From here, the track climbs over a headland behind Separation Point, where there is a worthwhile side-track to visit a seal colony (allow an extra hour).

The main track descends to the campsite at Mutton Cove. At the south end of the cove, it climbs around a rocky headland to reach Anapai Bay and its campsite. Another low, forested saddle separates Anapai Bay from Totaranui, where a substantial family campground exists, with a separate area for trampers.

Totaranui to Awaroa Hut (22 bunks)
2–2.5 hours, 7.1 km

After a walk down the lengthy golden beach of Totaranui, the track resumes, crossing a headland above Skinner Point to reach Goat Bay. While there is no campsite at Goat Bay, the next beach, Waiharakeke, does have one. From Waiharakeke Bay, the track crosses a substantial headland to the north end of Awaroa Inlet, the largest in Abel Tasman National Park. The 25-minute crossing of this inlet should be chanced only two hours either side of low tide; if in doubt, wait. Awaroa Hut lies on the far side of the inlet.

Awaroa Hut to Bark Bay Hut (34 bunks)
4.5–5 hours, 13.5 km

From Awaroa, the track skirts an area of private land and climbs over Tonga Saddle, reaching Onetahuti, or Tonga Roadstead, after a descent on the far side. Another tidal inlet here must be crossed three hours either side of low tide. Tonga Island and its marine reserve lie offshore. Two campsites exist on the pleasant curve of Onetahuti, the second near the site of a historic granite quarry.

Beyond the quarry site, the track once again climbs over another forested headland, descending to Bark Bay on the far side. Like Awaroa and Onetahuti, Bark Bay has a tidal inlet, but this one can be bypassed on a high-tide track. Bark Bay Hut is at the southern end of the inlet.

Bark Bay Hut to Anchorage Hut (34 bunks)
4 hours, 11.5 km

From the hut, the track skirts the shore of Bark Bay, then plunges back into the bush around South Head. From here, the track remains inland for some kilometres, descending to cross a substantial footbridge over the Falls River. En route, diversions along side-tracks to Sandfly Bay and a lookout over Frenchman Bay are both possible. At Torrent Bay the track reaches the coast again. For those wanting to walk directly to Anchorage Hut, the inlet at Torrent Bay can be crossed within two hours of low tide. However, the high-tide route around Torrent Bay passes one of the track's highlights: a 20-minute side-trip to Cleopatras Pool, an inviting – though chilly – swimming spot among the boulders of the Torrent River.

Anchorage Hut to Marahau 4 hours, 12.4 km

Anchorage is one of the most popular parts of Abel Tasman, and the hut here is the newest in the park. Here, sea-kayakers, yachties and walkers all congregate in a delightfully sheltered bay. If time allows, spend a day wandering the tracks around Pitt Head and the exquisite Te Pukatea Bay – arguably the most appealing of all the beaches in the park (allow 90 minutes).

South of Anchorage Hut, the main coastal track crosses another forested saddle, descending to the sea beyond Yellow Point. Side-tracks en route divert to campsites at Watering Cove, Observation Beach and Akersten Bay.

Beyond, the track skirts Stilwell Bay, reaching campsites at Apple Tree and Tinline bays. The track concludes at the Marahau carpark, where there are picnic tables, a shelter, a phone and information panels.

Yellow Point, Akersten Bay

Grade Easy

Maps Topo50 BP25 Motueka, BN25 Totaranui; Abel Tasman National Park Map

Access The northern end of the track begins at Wainui Inlet, 21 km from Takaka, in Golden Bay. Another option is to start from Totaranui (32 km from Takaka), reached via a winding, unsealed road past Wainui Inlet, or by water taxi from Marahau. The southern end of the track begins at Marahau (67 km from Nelson), where there is a campground, motel and cabin accommodation, a shop and several companies that operate guided sea-kayaking trips. Both ends are serviced by public transport, and the main beaches can be reached by water taxi. For an extra fee, water taxis will also transport your pack. Respect areas of private land by staying on the track.

Huts and campsites Huts and camping areas must be pre-booked (carry your own cooker and fuel). All huts cost $32/night and campsites $14/night, with youths aged under 18 free (but booking still required). Campsites exist at Whariwharangi, Mutton Cove, Anapai Bay, Totaranui, Waiharakeke Bay, Awaroa, Onetahuti, Tonga Quarry, Bark Bay, Torrent Bay, Anchorage, Te Pukatea Bay, Watering Cove, Observation Beach, Akersten Bay, Apple Tree Bay, Coquille Bay and Tinline Bay. All campsites have toilets and water supplies, and a few have cooking shelters.

Information and booking Nelson Visitor Centre, 79 Trafalgar Street, Nelson, tel: 0800 NZ GREAT WALKS (0800 694 732), email: greatwalks@doc.govt.nz, website: www.greatwalks.co.nz

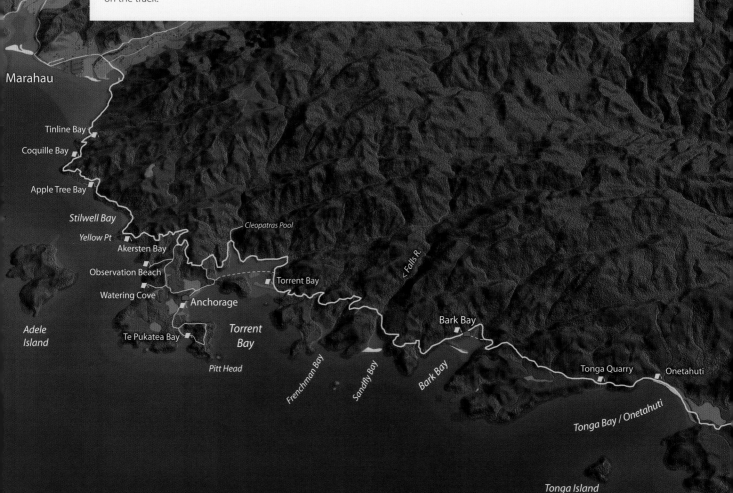

Marahau

Tinline Bay

Coquille Bay

Apple Tree Bay

Stilwell Bay

Yellow Pt

Akersten Bay

Cleopatras Pool

Observation Beach

Watering Cove

Anchorage

Te Pukatea Bay

Adele Island

Torrent Bay

Pitt Head

Torrent Bay

< Falls R.

Frenchman Bay

Sandfly Bay

Bark Bay

Bark Bay

Tonga Quarry

Onetahuti

Tonga Bay / Onetahuti

Tonga Island

Golden Bay

Pohara

Tata Beach

Wainui Inlet

Wainui Bay

Whariwharangi

Whariwharangi Bay

Awaroa Inlet

Totaranui

Awaroa

Waiharakeke Bay

Mutton Cove

Goat Bay

Totaranui

Anapai Bay

Mutton Cove

Skinner Pt

Separation Point

Awaroa Bay

Tonga Saddle

NORTH

HEAPHY TRACK
KAHURANGI NATIONAL PARK 4–6 DAYS

At 78 km, the Heaphy Track is the longest of the Great Walks, and possibly the most varied. Beginning in Golden Bay, and ending near Karamea at the northern extent of the West Coast, the well-benched and well-graded track passes through an extraordinary number of different ecosystems. The track climbs through the beech-dominated Aorere Valley to Perry Saddle and beyond to the subalpine moorlands of the Gouland and Mackay downs. Then it drops into the Heaphy Valley, descending from subalpine forests into the subtropical lowlands surrounding the Heaphy River. For many trampers the coastline – studded with nikau palms and craggy headlands, and pounded by vigorous West Coast surf – forms the highlight of the trip.

In historic times, Maori almost certainly used a route between the Heaphy and Aorere rivers, and as early as 500 years ago had an established settlement at the mouth of the Heaphy River. Although artist and explorer Charles Heaphy lent his name to the Heaphy Track, he only walked its coastal stretch as part of a journey in 1846. Two miners first crossed the route now followed by the Heaphy Track in 1859, followed soon afterward by explorer James Mackay in 1860. Through Mackay's advocacy, the Heaphy Track was first blazed and established over the next few years.

When the New Zealand Forest Service (NZFS) began promoting the area as Northwest Nelson Forest Park in the mid-1960s, the Heaphy Track was overgrown and its few existing huts badly needed to be replaced or upgraded. NZFS rangers began a major upgrade of the track, and several new huts were constructed over ensuing years. By the time the Northwest Nelson Forest Park was gazetted in 1970, the Heaphy had begun to attract trampers in their thousands. Since DOC took over in 1987, the Heaphy Track has gained Great Walk status, ensuring its popularity. Trampers can walk the track in either direction, although the east–west route is described here.

Mountain bikers can ride the Heaphy during the off-peak season, from the beginning of May until the end of September. Upgrading of the track in recent years has seen new huts, a gravelled and better-drained track surface, and bridges wide enough for mountain bikes. Because of the track's hardened surface, it is recommended that trampers wear comfortable, lightweight boots.

Brown Hut (16 bunks) to Perry Saddle Hut (28 bunks, woodburner, gas cookers)
5–6 hours, 17.5 km

The eastern end of the Heaphy Track begins at Brown Hut, located near the road end. Beyond the hut, the track soon crosses the Brown River on a footbridge, then begins a slow, steady ascent through beech forest onto a ridge above the Aorere River. After about 90 minutes, a side-track branches off to Shakespeare Flat, beside the Aorere River. The main trail continues to zigzag slowly uphill, reaching Aorere Shelter after a further two-and-a-half hours. From here, the track sidles around Brown Hill, where there is a lookout at Flanagans Corner (the track's highest point at 915 m). After another 30 minutes, the track reaches Perry Saddle Hut.

Coastal section of the Heaphy Track ROB BROWN

Perry Saddle Hut to Gouland Downs Hut (8 bunks, woodburner) 2 hours, 7 km

Soon after crossing Perry Saddle, the Heaphy Track begins to sidle on the true left of Perry Creek, crossing several side streams en route. After about an hour the valley begins to open out onto the expansive Gouland Downs. Here, red tussock grasslands mingle with other subalpine plants in rolling terrain dissected by numerous streams. En route, you pass one of the Heaphy's landmarks: a pole decorated with old discarded boots.

The track meanders towards Cave Brook, which is crossed on a footbridge about 10 minutes from Gouland Downs Hut. This is the smallest and oldest hut on the track.

Gouland Downs Hut to Saxon Hut (16 bunks, woodburner, gas cookers) 1.5 hours, 5.4 km

Limestone arches, small caves and small waterfalls near Gouland Downs Hut are all worth exploring. Beyond the hut, the track crosses the northern reaches of the Gouland Downs and enters the headwaters of Saxon River shortly before reaching Saxon Hut.

Saxon Hut to James Mackay Hut (28 bunks, woodburner, gas cookers) 3 hours, 11.8 km

From Saxon Hut the track traverses easy terrain beside the Saxon River before beginning a gentle climb around the forested slopes of Mt Teddy. Here, you edge onto the Mackay Downs, a flattish subalpine expanse similar to the Gouland Downs but less open, and with larger pockets of forest. Several creeks are crossed en route. James Mackay Hut, set on a terrace above the track, offers glimpses of the Tasman Sea and the mouth of the Heaphy River.

James Mackay Hut to Lewis Hut (20 bunks, woodburner, gas cookers) 3.5–4 hours, 12.5 km

From James Mackay Hut the track essentially descends a broad, prominent ridge that divides the Lewis and Heaphy rivers. Open beech forest dominates at first, but is replaced increasingly by denser, more diverse podocarp–broadleaf forests as you lose altitude. By the time trampers arrive at Lewis Hut, located near the junction of the Lewis and Heaphy rivers, nikau palms begin to lend the forest a subtropical look.

Lewis Hut to Heaphy Hut (32 bunks, woodburner, gas cookers) 2.5–3 hours, 8 km

At Lewis Hut, the track crosses first the Lewis River, then the Heaphy River, on large footbridges. Downstream, it curls around a major bend in the river beneath prominent limestone bluffs. Much of the rest of the section passes through lowland podocarp forest near or beside the Heaphy River. After about an hour, another footbridge crosses the Gunner River. Be aware that after heavy rain parts of the track can flood.

Nikau palms appear in increasing numbers until, near Heaphy Hut, they dominate the forest. Set 500 m back from the beach, Heaphy Hut overlooks the mouth of the Heaphy River. The impressive limestone bulk of Heaphy Bluff looms over the north bank of the river, with surf rolling in from the Tasman Sea. In summer, the sandflies are ferocious.

Heaphy Hut to Kohaihai River mouth
5–6 hours, 16.2 km

The last day's walk of the Heaphy Track provides a rare opportunity to stroll a wild, natural coastline, unblemished by past human activity. The track alternates between the forest and several beaches, crossing prominent streams that drain the nearby Gunner Downs.

A shelter exists at Katipo Creek. Some of the beach sections – notably at Crayfish Point – can be dangerous at mid- to high tide, when it is prudent to wait for low tide or use the high-tide track.

Beyond Scotts Beach, the track begins its only significant climb of the day, reaching a good lookout point some 160 m above the sea. Beyond, the track descends to the delightfully tea-coloured waters of the Kohaihai River, one of the most scenic points on the entire walk.

After crossing the Kohaihai on a footbridge, the track sidles above the river to conclude at Kohaihai Shelter, where there is a carpark, picnic tables, information panels and a phone.

Grade Medium

Maps Topo50 BP23 Gouland Downs; Kahurangi National Park Map

Access Brown Hut is accessible from Collingwood in Golden Bay (28 km). Kohaihai lies 15 km north of Karamea on the West Coast. As the ends of the track lie more than 460 km apart by road, using public transport is recommended. It's possible to fly, or take a bus or taxi.

Huts and campsites Huts and campsites must be pre-booked. Huts cost $32/night and campsites $14/night, with youths aged under 18 free (but booking still required). Designated campsites exist at all seven huts, and at Aorere Shelter, Katipo Creek Shelter, Scotts Beach and Kohaihai.

Information and booking Nelson Visitor Centre, 79 Trafalgar Street, Nelson, tel: 0800 NZ GREAT WALKS (0800 694 732), email: greatwalks@doc.govt.nz, website: www.greatwalks.co.nz

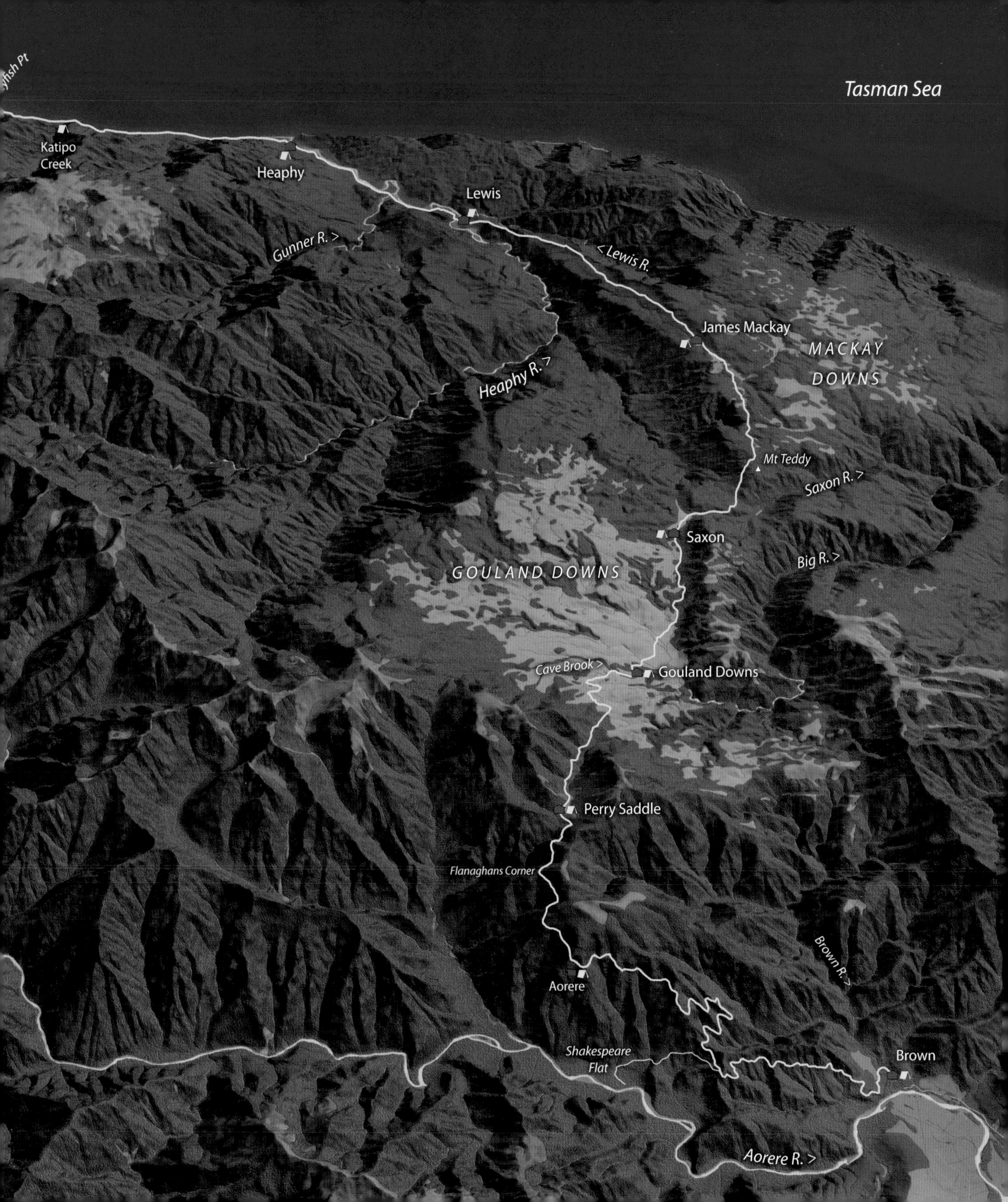

Tasman Sea

Katipo
Creek

Heaphy

Lewis

Gunner R. >

< Lewis R.

James Mackay

*MACKAY
DOWNS*

Heaphy R. >

▵ *Mt Teddy*

Saxon R. >

Saxon

Big R. >

GOULAND DOWNS

Cave Brook >

Gouland Downs

Perry Saddle

Flanaghans Corner

Brown R. >

Aorere

*Shakespeare
Flat*

Brown

Aorere R. >

WANGAPEKA TRACK
KAHURANGI NATIONAL PARK 4–6 DAYS

During the halcyon days of nineteenth-century gold-rush New Zealand, hopeful prospectors extensively searched much country previously probed only by Maori and Pakeha explorers. The mountains of northwest Nelson, now part of Kahurangi National Park, were one place where miners did strike some of the precious metal, although rarely in sufficient quantities for a lasting industry. Gold was first found in the Wangapeka in 1859, prompting the government to build a track connecting the valley with the West Coast. Progress was patchy, and the full track was not completed until 1899. Sections of the track destroyed in the 1929 Murchison Earthquake were rebuilt by unemployed men during the 1930s Depression.

Not only does the 59 km Wangapeka Track take trampers across a historic gold-mining route, but it also traverses the breadth of Kahurangi National Park from east to west. Crossing two passes, both above 1000 m, the well-benched and well-graded track traverses the headwaters of several attractively forested valleys, including the Wangapeka, Karamea, Taipo and Little Wanganui.

Despite being something of a classic tramp, the track has declined in popularity in recent years, and now DOC maintains the western part less frequently. As a consequence, it can sometimes be blocked by sections of wind-fall after storms. The eastern side of the track as far as Wangapeka Saddle is regularly maintained, but of tramping track standard, with sections of mud, tree roots and steep sections.

Trampers find accommodation in several comfortable modern huts and one historic hut. Although the track can be walked in either direction, the east–west route is described here. Highlights include the narrow gorges of both the Wangapeka and Little Wanganui, the historic Cecil King Hut, Saxon Falls, the views from Little Wanganui Saddle, and the chance of seeing blue ducks.

Rolling River to Kings Creek Hut (20 bunks, wood-burner) 3–4 hours, 11.4 km

Beyond the Rolling River carpark, the track soon crosses a footbridge over the Rolling River. From here, it follows the true right bank of the Wangapeka most of the way to Kings Creek Hut, crossing several bridged tributaries en route. A large slip in 2012 partially dammed the Wangapeka River, creating a small lake. Don't pause on the slip debris, and take care negotiating the marked route around the lake.

Views of the rugged Mt Patriarch, on the opposite side of the valley, open out in places. Some of the beech forest is still regenerating from fires, which were lit during the days when the valley was used for sheep grazing. At the junction of Kiwi Stream, the track crosses a swingbridge to the true left, reaching Kings Creek Hut after a further 40 minutes.

Kings Creek Hut to Stone Hut (12 bunks, wood-burner) 2.5–3 hours, 8.3 km

Five minutes beyond Kings Creek Hut is the historic Cecil King Hut, a shelter with more character than an old boot. Built in 1935 by prospector Cecil King, who visited the valley until his death in 1981, the hut was beautifully restored in 1991. Those who spend a night in the four-bunker often comment on the feeling of peace it evokes. Beyond Cecil King Hut, the track heads up the North Branch of the Wangapeka, climbing steadily up the valley as the river

Historic Cecil King Hut

narrows. A bridge leads to the true right bank about 30 minutes before reaching Stone Hut.

Stone Hut to Helicopter Flat Hut (12 bunks, woodburner) via Wangapeka Saddle 4–5 hours, 10.4 km

From Stone Hut the track begins to climb out of the Wangapeka Valley, crossing a large slip en route. Through beech trees the track zigzags up to crest the 1009 m Wangapeka Saddle, which due to forest cover offers disappointingly few views. A track to Biggs Tops branches off at the saddle.

The main Wangapeka Track begins a descent into the headwaters of the Karamea River, which must be forded a few times or avoided on a wet-weather track (adding an extra 20 minutes). Waters Creek is the last side stream crossed before Helicopter Flat Hut (when the creek is in flood, use the three-wire bridge upstream). Helicopter Flat, situated on a grassy terrace above the infant Karamea River and set among copses of beech trees, is a pleasant place to spend the night.

Helicopter Flat Hut to Taipo Hut (16 bunks, woodburner) 3.5–4 hours, 8.6 km

From Helicopter Flat, trampers have two options. The main Wangapeka Track sidles above the Karamea River, past a historic surveyors' site at Brough's Tabernacle, and into the Taipo catchment. From here, it follows the Taipo River to Taipo Hut.

A longer but more interesting track leads over a low saddle into Lost Valley Creek and down to the new 12-bunk Trevor Carter Hut. From the hut, two tracks lead up the Karamea Valley to join the main Wangapeka Track; one passes near the impressive Saxon Falls en route.

Taipo Hut occupies a sunny bank, with good views towards Little Wanganui Saddle and the ranges above it.

Taipo Hut to Belltown Manunui Hut (10 bunks, woodburner) via Little Wanganui Saddle
6.5–8 hours, 10.2 km

From Taipo Hut, the track climbs gradually to the headwaters of the Taipo River, reaching Stag Flat Shelter (2 bunks) after about 60 minutes. From here, the track climbs 200 m steeply up an impressive face onto Little Wanganui Saddle (1087 m), the highest point on the track. On a good day there are fine views of the mountains either side.

The far side of the saddle offers a gentler descent, at first, passing the Saddle Lakes before entering the forest once again. Steeper travel leads down into the Little Wanganui Valley. The Wangapeka Bivvy (2 bunks) lies 150 m from the track, just before a footbridge is crossed to the true right. The track leads down the valley, climbing around a gorge past Tangent Creek, until reaching the river once again at Smith Creek. Belltown Manunui Hut, built in 2000, occupies the site of a historic hut.

Belltown Manunui Hut to Little Wanganui
3–3.5 hours, 10 km

From Belltown Hut the Wangapeka Track essentially follows the true right of the Little Wanganui River to the open grass of Gilmore Clearing. Part of the remainder of the track diverts away from the river, before rejoining it for the last leg to the Wangapeka Road carpark. En route, there are good swimming holes in the river.

Wangapeka River

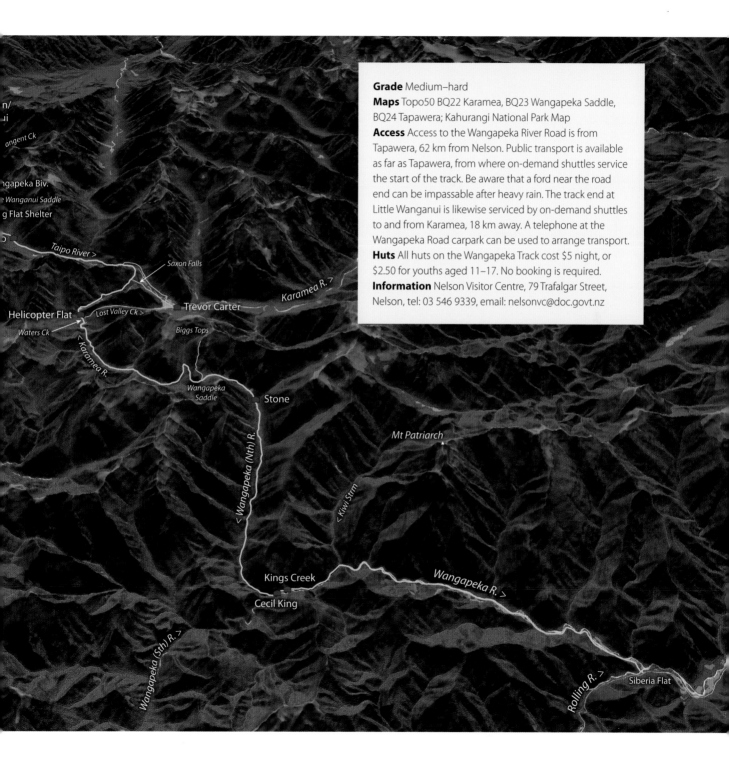

Grade Medium–hard

Maps Topo50 BQ22 Karamea, BQ23 Wangapeka Saddle, BQ24 Tapawera; Kahurangi National Park Map

Access Access to the Wangapeka River Road is from Tapawera, 62 km from Nelson. Public transport is available as far as Tapawera, from where on-demand shuttles service the start of the track. Be aware that a ford near the road end can be impassable after heavy rain. The track end at Little Wanganui is likewise serviced by on-demand shuttles to and from Karamea, 18 km away. A telephone at the Wangapeka Road carpark can be used to arrange transport.

Huts All huts on the Wangapeka Track cost $5 night, or $2.50 for youths aged 11–17. No booking is required.

Information Nelson Visitor Centre, 79 Trafalgar Street, Nelson, tel: 03 546 9339, email: nelsonvc@doc.govt.nz

Taipo River >

Saxon Falls

Trevor Carter

Karamea R. >

Helicopter Flat

Lost Valley Ck >

Waters Ck

< Karamea R.

Biggs Tops

Wangapeka Saddle

Stone

< Wangapeka (Nth) R.

Mt Patriarch

< Kiwi Strm

Kings Creek

Cecil King

Wangapeka R. >

Wangapeka (Sth) R. >

Rolling R. >

Siberia Flat

angent Ck

ngapeka Biv.

Wanganui Saddle

g Flat Shelter

MT ARTHUR AND THE TABLELANDS
KAHURANGI NATIONAL PARK 2 DAYS

One of Kahurangi's most appealing overnight tramps is the circuit up to Mt Arthur, over Gordons Pyramid to the Tablelands, and then out along the Flora Valley. It has a bit of everything: mountains, tussock tops, expansive views, good tracks and huts, pleasant forest, bubbling brooks and distinctive rock shelters. Native birds are plentiful, too, thanks to the predator-control efforts of a local conservation group, Friends of the Flora – increasing the likelihood you'll encounter kaka, kakariki and blue duck.

Long before the Tablelands were protected, graziers and gold miners sought to wrest a living from the area. One of the huts, Salisbury Lodge, is named after John Salisbury, who first farmed the area in the 1870s, driving sheep and cattle up the Graham Valley, onto the Tablelands and beyond into the Cobb Valley. Grazing continued until the 1950s.

Gold, first discovered on the Tablelands in 1865, proved a shorter-lasting enterprise and was never particularly profitable. During the 1930s Depression, government subsidies enticed out-of-work men from the cities to try their luck at mining the area again, but they found little except toil, bitterly cold winters and scorching summers. In the 1960s, the area was protected as part of Northwest Nelson Forest Park, and later, in 1996, became Kahurangi National Park.

Flora carpark to Mt Arthur Hut (8 bunks, wood-burner) 1.5 hours, 4.2 km

Situated at the lofty altitude of 940 m, Flora carpark provides one of the easiest ways to reach the tops of Kahurangi National Park. Here, a shelter facing Mt Arthur provides information on the area's natural and human history. The wide track (once a vehicle track) climbs gently to a signposted track junction at Flora Saddle. Head left towards Mt Arthur Hut. More gentle climbing through beech forest leads into a section of mountain neinei and beyond to the hut, nestled near the bush edge.

Mt Arthur Hut to Mt Arthur summit 1.5–2 hours, 5 km; Mt Arthur summit to Salisbury Lodge (22 bunks, gas cooking and heating) via Gordons Pyramid 3.5–4 hours, 11 km

Behind Mt Arthur Hut, the track passes the last of the forest and emerges onto the tops. From here, a poled route leads through subalpine plants and across bands of interesting marble. Mt Arthur is honeycombed with caves and sinkholes, some of which are apparent from the track (beware that under winter snow sinkholes can be obscured).

A signpost indicates the turnoff to Gordons Pyramid, but if the day is fine, most trampers will first want to climb Mt Arthur. After more gentle travel, the ridge steepens, and poles lead through marble faces up onto the broad summit of Mt Arthur (1795 m). This is one of the finest viewpoints in Kahurangi, with the Tablelands prominent in the foreground.

Back at the track junction, poles lead across Horseshoe Basin, then up onto a gently climbing ridge that culminates in Gordons Pyramid. A tussock spur on the far side soon leads to the bush edge, where the track descends onto the Tablelands. After you emerge onto the first area of open tussock grasslands, Salisbury Lodge is only 20 minutes away.

Mt Arthur from Gordons Pyramid

Salisbury Lodge to Flora carpark via rock shelters and Flora Hut (12 bunks, open fire)
3.5–4.5 hours, 14 km

After a night at Salisbury Lodge, head north on the poled track leading into the Flora Valley. The rolling tussock expanses punctuated by patches of forest make delightfully easy tramping. A worthwhile diversion is the short side-trail to Salisbury or Dry Rock Shelter, the first encounter with several such shelters unique to Kahurangi. First developed by well-known NZFS ranger Max Polglaze, these open-air shelters have sleeping benches built under limestone rock overhangs, which provide protection from the rain.

Further along the main Flora Track, now in beech forest above Balloon Creek, you pass Growler, a small open shelter built under an overhang beside the track. Next comes Lower Gridiron, the most impressive of the shelters. Finally, there is Upper Gridiron (reached via a five-minute side-track), which is an innovative three-bunk hut built into an overhang, using rock as one half of its roof.

Beyond the Gridiron shelters, the Flora Track meanders gently upwards to Flora Saddle, passing the two-roomed Flora Hut en route. Over recent years, members of the Nelson Tramping Club have restored the hut, a historic shelter originally built in 1928. From Flora Saddle, it's a 20-minute amble back to the Flora carpark.

Above *Tramper descending towards the Tablelands from Gordons Pyramid*
Left *Lower Gridiron rock shelter*

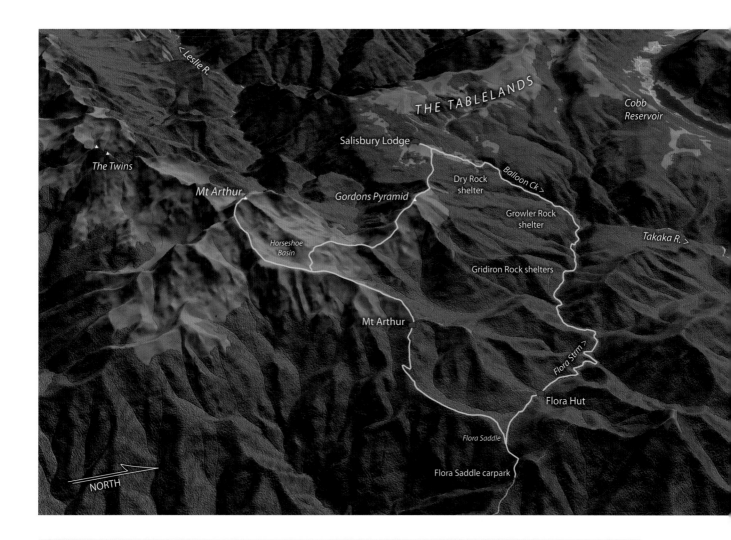

Grade Medium
Maps Topo50 BQ24 Tapawera; Kahurangi National Park Map
Access Flora carpark is 75 km from Nelson and 36 km from Motueka. Take the Motueka Valley Highway to Ngatimoti, then turn off onto Peninsular Road and head south on Motueka River West Bank Road; the Graham Valley Road branches off 5 km beyond. Slips have closed the Graham Valley Road for long periods in recent years, but at the time of writing (2015) access is possible. The last 6 km is very steep,

however, and unsealed, and during winter a four-wheel-drive vehicle is recommended. Alternatively, trampers can access the Tablelands from the Cobb Valley, using the track to Lake Peel and Balloon Hut.

Huts Mt Arthur Hut and Salisbury Lodge cost $15/night, or $7.50 for youths aged 11–17. No booking is required. Staying in Flora Hut and the rock shelters is free.

Information Nelson Visitor Centre, 79 Trafalgar Street, Nelson, tel: 03 546 9339, email: nelsonvc@doc.govt.nz

LAKE ANGELUS
NELSON LAKES NATIONAL PARK 2–3 DAYS

A tramp to Lake Angelus offers a concentrated sample of all that is best in Nelson Lakes National Park: the expansive tops of Robert Ridge, a large alpine lake, the tumbling Hukere Stream and the bush-clad fringes of Lake Rotoiti. The tramp can be combined with the Travers–Sabine Circuit (see page 38), but a more leisurely trip, involving a couple of nights at Angelus Hut, often proves more rewarding.

While the section along Robert Ridge is generally not difficult, the terrain here is extremely exposed to bad weather, and in winter will require good alpine skills and equipment. Angelus Hut is very popular during the summer season, and requires booking.

Mt Robert Road to Bushline Hut (14 bunks, wood-burner) 1.5–2 hours, 5 km

From the carpark, the trail to Bushline Hut – known as Paddys Track – is clearly signposted and skirts above the artificially low bushline of Mt Robert, crossing in and out of numerous guts. This face of Mt Robert, burnt from the days when it was grazed, is only very slowly regaining a cover of native plants. The track enters forest again for a short stretch.

Shortly after crossing Robert Stream, the track begins to climb in a series of zigzags, rounds the broad shoulder of Pt 1098 m, then begins the last ascent to Bushline Hut. Superbly located, the hut has views over St Arnaud and Lake Rotoiti.

Bushline Hut to Angelus Hut (28 bunks, wood-burner) via Robert Ridge 4–6 hours, 14 km

From Bushline Hut, the well-graded Paddys Track leads up a broad, rounded spur, soon passing the private Kea Hut (a restored historic ski hut). Be sure to carry plenty of water as there is none available along the route.

Paddys Track joins the main Robert Ridge Route a few hundred metres south of Mt Robert itself. From here, a well-cairned and well-poled route traverses the crest of Robert Ridge, passing several large alpine basins, all filled with small tarns. In the 2nd Basin lie the buildings of the now-defunct Mt Robert ski-field, a victim of too many lean winters.

The route skirts beneath the western side of the craggy Julius Summit, before regaining the ridge again above the 4th Basin. The vegetable sheep, a curious alpine plant bearing a passing resemblance to a mound of wool, offers a botanical diversion in many places.

After passing the route to Speargrass Hut on the right, climb a little further to the crest of the ridge overlooking the basin dominated by Lake Angelus. Follow the poles down the steep spur and then walk around the edge of the lake to reach the sizeable hut perched on a ledge above the lake.

For those staying an extra night here, worthwhile side-trips include Hinapouri Tarn, Angelus Peak and Sunset Saddle.

Angelus Hut to Coldwater Hut (12 bunks, open fire) via Hukere Stream 5–6 hours, 12 km

From Angelus Hut, a poled route leads down into the head of Hukere Stream, which is characterised by cascades and waterfalls. After a steep, rocky descent, the Cascade Track begins at the bush edge. Shortly downstream is a very pleasant clearing offering good camping. Beyond, the track down Hukere Stream descends through typically mossy

Angelus Hut and Lake Angelus

beech forest, eventually emerging onto the flats of the Travers Valley.

Cross Hukere Stream on a sizeable footbridge, then head north on the Lower Travers Valley Track leading down the true left of the Travers River. Flat, easy tramping leads to Coldwater Hut, situated above a beach at the head of Lake Rotoiti.

Coldwater Hut to Mt Robert Road
3–4 hours, 10 km

From Coldwater Hut, the Lakeside Track skirts the slopes on the western side of Lake Rotoiti, providing pleasant, undulating tramping. Whisky Falls offers a diversion after about 90 minutes. Where the lake begins to broaden, the track departs the shore and heads through flattish, forested terrain to end at Mt Robert Road, about 20 minutes' walk from the upper carpark.

Lake Rotoroa

Sunset
Saddle

Maniniaro / Angelus Pk

Hinapouri
Tarn

Lake
Angelus

Angelus

to Speargrass Hut

Julius
Summit

4th
Basin

R O B E R T   R I D G

3rd
Basin

< Hukere Strm

2nd
Basin

former
skifield

Cascade Track

Lower Travers Valley Track

Travers R. >

Coldwater

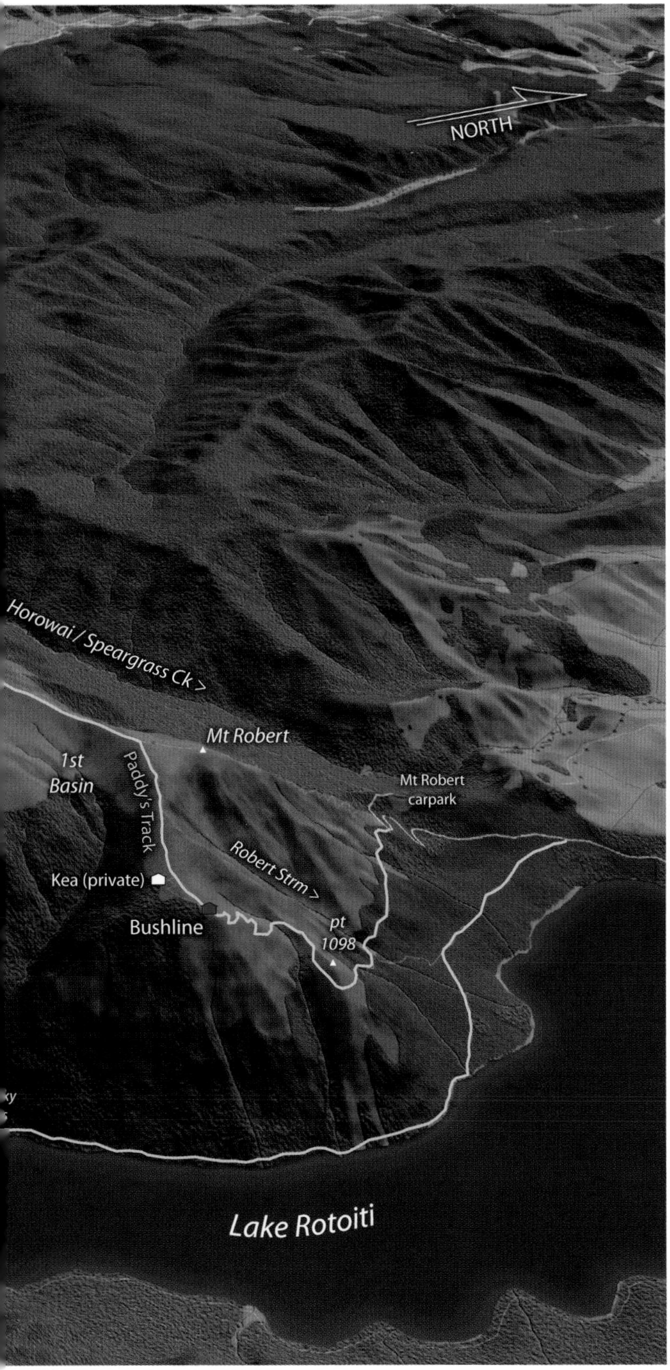
NORTH
Horowai / Speargrass Ck >
Mt Robert
1st Basin
Paddy's Track
Mt Robert carpark
Robert Strm >
Kea (private)
Bushline
pt 1098
Lake Rotoiti

Grade Medium–hard
Maps Topo50 BR24 Kawatiri, BS24 Mount Robert; Nelson Lakes National Park Map
Access St Arnaud is 87 km from Nelson. From St Arnaud, head west along State Highway 63 for 2 km, then turn left onto Mt Robert Road and drive to the carpark, where there is a shelter and toilets. During the summer months, buses and shuttles service St Arnaud.
Huts Angelus Hut costs $20/night, or $10/night for youths aged 11–17. Between late November and 30 April, bookings are required. Bushline and Coldwater huts are $5/night, or $2.50 for youths aged 11–17, and do not require booking.
Information DOC Nelson Lakes Visitor Centre, View Road, St Arnaud, tel: 03 521 1806, email: nelsonlakesvc@doc.govt.nz

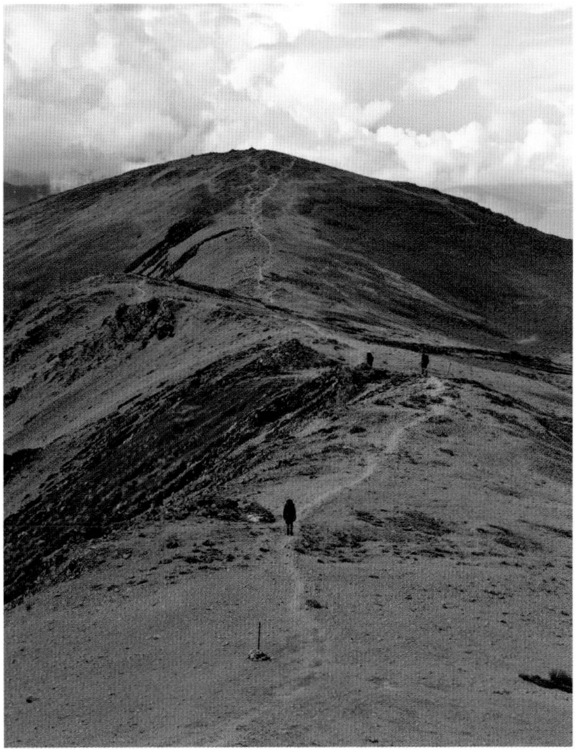

Trampers on Robert Ridge

TRAVERS–SABINE CIRCUIT
NELSON LAKES NATIONAL PARK 5–7 DAYS

Prior to the late 1980s, Nelson Lakes National Park remained largely the domain of New Zealand trampers, but it was only a matter of time before the secret leaked out to the wider world. Nelson Lakes is a park where you can have a gentle introduction to the Southern Alps, where there are dazzling alpine lakes, U-shaped valleys, good tracks and ample, substantial huts. The 85 km Travers–Sabine Circuit (or 103 km including a side-trip to Blue Lake) is now well established as a destination for overseas hikers, and is the most popular of the park's longer multi-day tramps. For those who prefer to eschew crowds, there are many delightful places to camp en route.

Walking the track in any season has merit: summer is good for swimming and alpine flowers; during autumn fungi are at their most prolific; in winter trampers will enjoy alpine environs (if appropriately equipped with ice axes and crampons); and over spring the forests take on fresh, vivid greens. Be aware that after snowfalls avalanches can be a significant risk in the West Sabine, Hopeless Creek and over Travers Saddle. If in doubt, check the latest conditions with DOC at St Arnaud. For those wanting to shorten the trip, water taxis are available on both Lake Rotoiti and Lake Rotoroa (book these in advance of your trip).

Lake Rotoiti to Lakehead Hut (28 bunks, wood-burner) 3 hours, 12 km

From Kerr Bay on Lake Rotoiti, the track begins on a wide gravelled path skirting the eastern shores of the lake. Over recent years DOC has undertaken major ecological restoration work (the Rotoiti Nature Recovery Project) in the forests on this side of the lake, and birdlife abounds. The track largely stays in the forest, crossing several streams, but emerges onto the lakeshore in a few places. Lakehead Hut occupies a position overlooking the head of Lake Rotoiti, about 10 minutes' walk from a nearby jetty.

Lakehead Hut to John Tait Hut (27 bunks, wood-burner) 4.5–5 hours, 15 km

From Lakehead Hut, the track heads up the Travers Valley through a mixture of grassy flats and beech forest, crossing a footbridge to the true left after about 90 minutes. Beyond here, the valley narrows, with views of both the St Arnaud Range and the distant Mt Travers in places. After crossing the footbridge over Hopeless Creek, you pass a side-track to Hopeless Hut. Keeping on the main track, some climbing ensues as it ascends above a confined section of the river. Soon after the track nears the river again, John Tait Hut is reached.

John Tait Hut to Upper Travers Hut (24 bunks, woodburner) 3 hours, 8 km

Thirty minutes up the valley from John Tait Hut, the track reaches Cupola Creek, where another side-track branches off to Cupola Hut. Beyond the junction, the track climbs steadily around a gorged section of the Travers River. A short diversion to the 20 m-high Travers Falls is worthwhile. After about another 90 minutes' walking, the track crosses to the true right of the Travers, then begins a steady 30–40-minute ascent into the upper valley. Upper Travers Hut occupies a magnificent site beneath grand mountains.

Opposite *Evening over Lake Rotoroa from Sabine Hut*

Upper Travers Hut to West Sabine Hut (30 bunks, woodburner) via Travers Saddle 6–9 hours, 11 km

From Upper Travers Hut, the track crosses the Travers River (on a footbridge) for the last time. From here, the route over Travers Saddle is poled, climbing 450 m up moderately steep slopes beneath Mt Travers, and reaching the high, broad pass (1787 m) after 90 minutes or so.

On the western side of the pass, a steep, rocky descent leads into the East Branch of the Sabine River. After passing through a small patch of stunted beech forest, the route descends beside a scree gut, zigzagging through forest. Where the route reaches the East Sabine, the walking becomes flatter and easier. Soon, the track crosses to the true left on another footbridge, over an impressively deep chasm. West Sabine Hut is located about 10 minutes up from the junction of the West and East branches of the Sabine.

West Sabine Hut to Blue Lake Hut (16 bunks, woodburner) 3–3.5 hours, 9 km each way

Although a side-trip up to Blue Lake will add another day or two onto your trip, to miss this walk would be to miss one of the circuit's highlights. From West Sabine Hut, the track crosses to the true left of the river, and from here the route to Blue Lake heads upriver. It's a long, slow ascent through forest in the West Sabine Valley, breaking out to views of the waterfalls and mountains of the Mahanga Range after two to three hours. Beware of potential avalanche risk beyond here. The final push up to Blue Lake occurs through some delightful sections of mossy forest, with the river tumbling through attractive cascades. Blue Lake Hut lies about five minutes' walk from the enchantingly turquoise Blue Lake, which scientists believe may be the world's clearest fresh water.

West Sabine Hut to Sabine Hut (32 bunks, wood-burner) 5 hours, 17 km

Back at West Sabine Hut, the track downstream follows the true left of the Sabine River, descending gradually through forest and occasionally breaking out onto grassy river flats. About 40 minutes before Sabine Hut is reached, the track crosses a footbridge over the roaring Sabine Gorge to the true right. Sabine Hut occupies a pleasant spot near the shores of Lake Rotoroa, a larger version of neighbouring Lake Rotoiti.

Sabine Hut to Mt Robert Road via Speargrass Hut (12 bunks, woodburner) 7–8 hours, 22 km

From Sabine Hut, the track to Speargrass Hut climbs to Howard Saddle, then begins a sidle around the undulating forested flanks of Mt Cedric, crossing several small streams en route. From Sabine Hut it will take four to five hours, and much up and down travel, to reach Speargrass Hut, situated in a tussock clearing with fine views of Robert Ridge. After lunch at the hut, continue on the track, which soon descends into Speargrass Creek. About two hours after leaving the hut, the track begins to climb gradually, ending at the Mt Robert carpark some 30–40 minutes later.

Grade Medium–hard

Maps Topo50 BR24 Kawatiri, BS24 Mount Robert; Nelson Lakes National Park Map

Access St Arnaud is 87 km from Nelson. From St Arnaud, head west along State Highway 63 for 2 km, then turn left onto Mt Robert Road and drive to the carpark, where there is a shelter and toilets. During the summer months, buses and shuttles service St Arnaud.

Huts All huts cost $15/night, or $7.50 for youths aged 11–17. No booking is required.

Information DOC Nelson Lakes Visitor Centre, View Road, St Arnaud, tel: 03 521 1806, email: nelsonlakesvc@doc.govt.nz

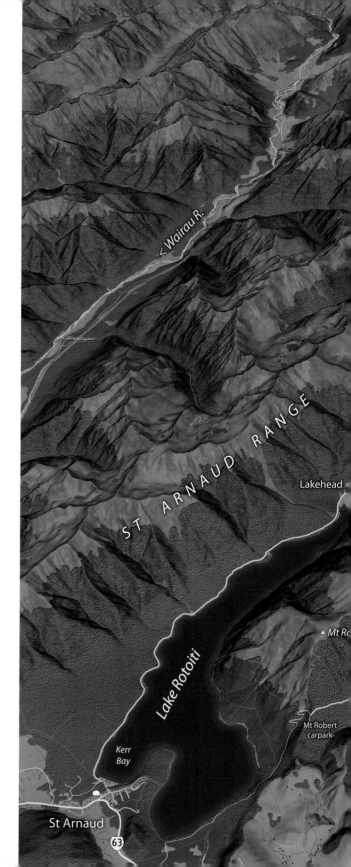

Rotopōhueroa / Lake Constance

Blue Lake

Travers
Saddle

E. Sabine R. >

< W. Sabine R.

MAHANGA RANGE

Upper Travers

Mt
Travers

Mt Cupola

West Sabine

Travers Falls

Cupola

John Tait

T R A V E R S   R A N G E

< Sabine R.

< D'Urville R.

Mt Hopeless

Hopeless

< Travers R.

Maniniaro / Angelus Pk

Mt Cedric

Sabine

Howard
Saddle

Lake Rotoroa

R O B E R T   R I D G E

Speargrass

< Te Horowai / Speargrass Ck

NORTH

LAKE DANIELL
LEWIS PASS SCENIC RESERVE 1–2 DAYS

An easier, more pleasant overnight tramp on the West Coast would be hard to find. The gentle, graded track, a spacious hut, stately beech forests, good fishing and a tranquil lake combine to make this tramp an enjoyable one for trampers of all abilities. Lake Daniell is a popular destination, particularly with school groups and families, but the hut is large, with two bunkrooms, and plenty of camping spots exist nearby. Those preferring solitude can always find refuge at the northern end of the lake, where there are other pleasant spots to camp.

Marble Hill Picnic Area to Manson–Nicholls Memorial Hut (24 bunks, woodburner) 3 hours, 8.4 km
The tramp begins from the carpark at the Marble Hill Picnic Area. Follow the well-graded and gravelled track for 10 minutes to The Sluice Box, a narrow marble canyon through which the sizeable Maruia River passes. Cross the footbridge over the river. From here, the track follows the true right bank of the Alfred River, passing through tall red beech forest at a gentle gradient.

Opposite where the sizeable Pell Stream tributary joins the Alfred River, a bench seat offers trampers a place to rest. Beyond here, the track branches up Frazer Stream and after a kilometre or so begins to climb gently over a forested lip to reach Lake Daniell. The hut lies a few minutes' walk away, on the southeastern edge of the lake.

Lake Daniell was formed by a landslide that spilled from a nearby peak, in an event similar to those that formed others in the area like Lake Christabel. Tragically, another landslide in 1974 destroyed a previous hut that used to occupy the lake's western shores, killing three of the occupants. The present hut is named after those who died – Brian and Sharon Manson, and Phil Nicholls. It has two rooms, each with 12 bunks, and a large kitchen.

Near the lake is a small jetty, the perfect place to appreciate the tranquillity of your surroundings. Both rainbow and brown trout offer possibilities for those interested in fishing.

Misty winter dawn at Lake Daniell

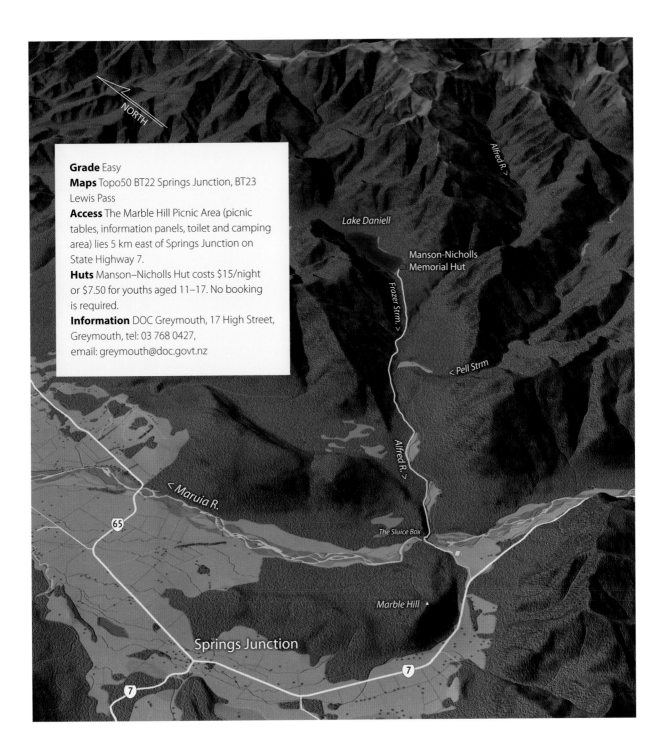

NORTH

Grade Easy

Maps Topo50 BT22 Springs Junction, BT23 Lewis Pass

Access The Marble Hill Picnic Area (picnic tables, information panels, toilet and camping area) lies 5 km east of Springs Junction on State Highway 7.

Huts Manson–Nicholls Hut costs $15/night or $7.50 for youths aged 11–17. No booking is required.

Information DOC Greymouth, 17 High Street, Greymouth, tel: 03 768 0427, email: greymouth@doc.govt.nz

Alfred R. >

Lake Daniell

Manson-Nicholls Memorial Hut

Frazer Strm. >

< Pell Strm

Alfred R. >

< Maruia R.

65

The Sluice Box

Marble Hill ▲

Springs Junction

7

7

KIRWANS REWARD CIRCUIT
VICTORIA FOREST PARK 3–4 DAYS

Set on a knoll high above the West Coast township of Reefton, Kirwans Hut offers grand views over the Southern Alps and the Victoria and Paparoa ranges. However, the main attraction of this tramp is the wealth of mining relics remaining from an intense period of gold extraction in the early twentieth century. In 1896, prospector William Kirwan discovered what was one of New Zealand's highest and remotest sources of quartz at about 1200 m above the Waitahu Valley. Extracting ore from Kirwans Reward Mine, as it came to be known, involved some ingenious engineering. A 1.5 km-long aerial cableway transported ore-filled buckets down a steep, forested hillside into Kirwans Creek, where a stamper battery crushed the quartz. Despite the expensive machinery and remoteness of the site, the mine proved profitable for a few short years between 1900 and 1906. Combined with tracks in the Murray Creek goldfields, the 40 km Kirwans Reward Circuit rates as one of the best historical tramps in New Zealand.

Capleston to Kirwans Hut (12 bunks, woodburner) 4–5 hours, 16 km

Aside from cattle, a tin shed and a few abandoned car bodies, there is not much to mark the former mining community of Capleston, which in the 1870s boasted some 1,000 residents and several pubs. From the carpark, follow Boatmans Creek on the true left side until you cross the swingbridge, from where the clearly marked track starts. The track initially follows an old road, before reaching a short tunnel (built to divert water by miners operating the nearby Fiery Cross and Just in Time mines). Once through the tunnel, the track crosses a swingbridge over Topfer Creek and heads upstream. Two more footbridges are crossed before the track begins to wind slowly uphill, following a gentle contour on an old bridle track that is easy on both limbs and lungs. Miners used packhorses on this track to service Kirwans Reward Mine.

About an hour before Kirwans Hut, pole silver beech begins to dominate the forest. Higher up, near the ridge crest, a signposted track finally branches off to Kirwans Hill. Five minutes further on, another signpost indicates the track to Kirwans Hut, reached after a short 10-minute uphill climb.

Partially surrounded by stunted beech forest, the attractive Kirwans Hut has views over the Inangahua Valley, the Paparoa Range and the distant peaks of the Southern Alps. Nearby Kirwans Hill, about 30–40 minutes' walk away (2 km each way), offers fine panoramas of the central Victoria Range.

Kirwans Hut to Montgomerie Hut (6 bunks, woodburner) 3.5–4 hours, 9 km

Once on the main track, take care to select the correct route leading to Montgomerie Hut. After a short distance, a side-track branches off to visit Kirwans Reward Mine, the site of once-intense activity. Here, stunted trees are slowly colonising substantial piles of diggings. Nearby, the remains of the aerial cableway span a steep gully – complete with two ore buckets still hanging in the breeze.

Back on the main track, you soon pass another clearing with the ruins of several miners' buildings. All that remains of Mrs Flannigan's boarding house is an iron bed, some glass bottles, abandoned tools and parts of a Shacklock stove.

In a series of zigzags the track descends a forested slope in the headwaters of Kirwans Creek. Perhaps the most

impressive remains of the aerial cableway are two large return wheels, one lying askew on the ground, the other threaded by a now-substantial beech tree. The cableway made ingenious use of gravity – laden ore buckets going downhill powered the uphill return of empty buckets.

At the bottom of the slope, the track reaches the Lord Brassey Stamper Battery, an impressive 15-stamper battery that has been magnificently restored in recent years.

After the ore was crushed and processed at the Lord Brassey Stamper Battery, any gold extracted was carried out by packhorse to Reefton. The tramp follows this same route, passing through mossy stands of red beech on the true right of Kirwans Creek to the Montgomerie River. Here, the track heads downstream, staying on the true right until reaching Montgomerie Hut. A good swimming hole in the Waitahu River lies just below the hut.

Montgomerie Hut to Capleston via Waitahu River
4–5 hours, 15 km

To complete the circuit back to Capleston, trampers simply follow a rough four-wheel-drive track down the true right of the Waitahu River to the road end at Gannons Bridge. This is an undemanding but not particularly scenic walk, with views of the open-cast Garvey Creek Coal Mine en route. From Gannons Bridge, a marked trail leads through a mixture of native forest and pine plantation and over a low ridge back to the carpark at Capleston. At times, this section of track is closed due to forestry activity, so check with DOC before your visit. Those who can make suitable transport arrangements are advised to take the option below.

Above *Kirwans Hut*

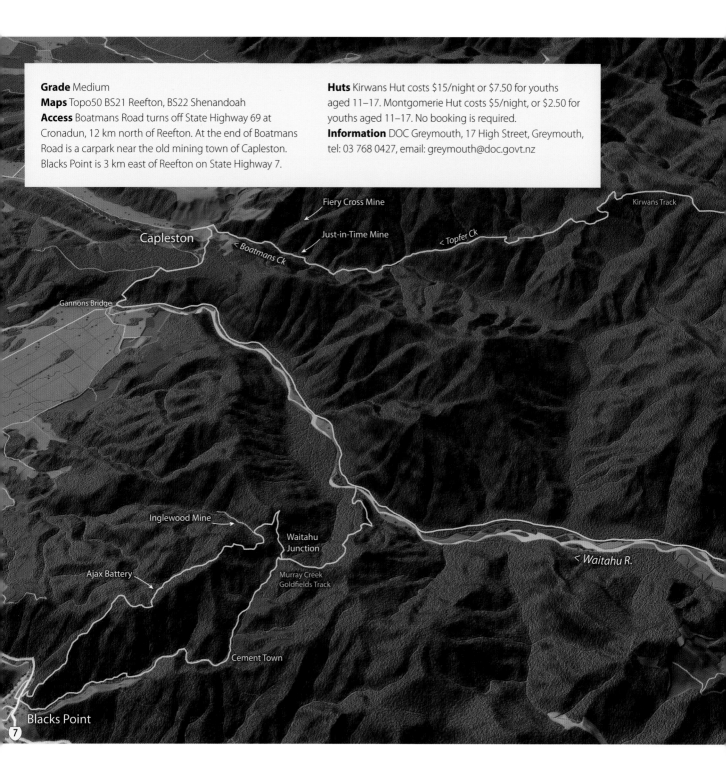

Grade Medium

Maps Topo50 BS21 Reefton, BS22 Shenandoah

Access Boatmans Road turns off State Highway 69 at Cronadun, 12 km north of Reefton. At the end of Boatmans Road is a carpark near the old mining town of Capleston. Blacks Point is 3 km east of Reefton on State Highway 7.

Huts Kirwans Hut costs $15/night or $7.50 for youths aged 11–17. Montgomerie Hut costs $5/night, or $2.50 for youths aged 11–17. No booking is required.

Information DOC Greymouth, 17 High Street, Greymouth, tel: 03 768 0427, email: greymouth@doc.govt.nz

Fiery Cross Mine

Just-in-Time Mine

Kirwans Track

Capleston

< Boatmans Ck

< Topfer Ck

Gannons Bridge

Inglewood Mine

Waitahu Junction

< Waitahu R.

Ajax Battery

Murray Creek Goldfields Track

Cement Town

Blacks Point

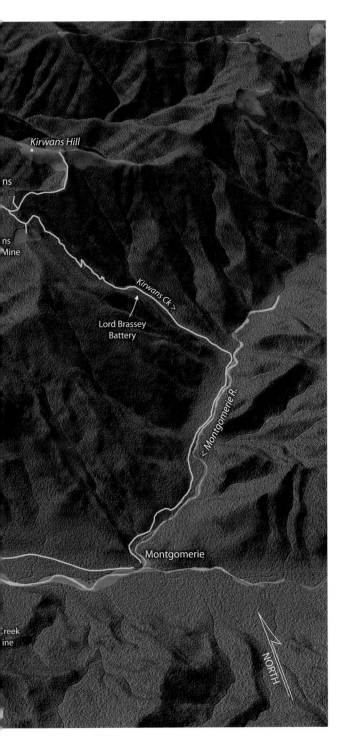

Montgomerie Hut to Blacks Point via Murray Creek Goldfields Track 4–5 hours, 15 km

About two hours along the Waitahu Valley track, it is possible to cross the river and link with the relic-littered Murray Creek Goldfields Track. The Murray brothers first discovered gold in the area in 1866, but significant mining did not occur until the 1870s, when some 200 claims were pegged out. Payable gold finally dwindled out in the 1920s, although coal was extracted from the area as late as the 1960s.

After crossing the Waitahu River, the track climbs steadily through beech forest to Waitahu Junction. From here, the quickest route to Blacks Point goes via the Cement Town Junction, but a more interesting option is to head past the Inglewood Junction and Ajax Battery. At the end of your tramp, the Blacks Point Museum is worth a visit.

Return wheel and bucket near head of Kirwans Creek

INLAND PACK TRACK
PAPAROA NATIONAL PARK 1–2 DAYS

One of the few recognised overnight tramps in the Paparoa National Park, the 27 km Inland Pack Track takes trampers among spectacular cliff-lined river valleys in the park's coastal limestone band. Festooned with subtropical nikau palms and mossy streams, the track connects the Fox River with the Pororari Valley. Prior to the 1920s, when a road was pushed past the formidable cliffs characterising the coast, the Inland Pack Track was the main route – a miners' track that had first been developed in 1867.

No huts exist on the track. Instead, most trampers opt to camp under the Ballroom Overhang, an impressive half-arch of limestone beside the Fox River, and one of the trip's highlights. Although the track can be enjoyed at any time of year, good river-crossing skills are necessary. Because water levels can rise extremely rapidly, start the trip only when rain is unlikely.

Tiromoana, State Highway 6, to Ballroom Overhang via Fox River 2–2.5 hours, 7 km

At Tiromoana, a short section of road leads from the highway to the point where the Inland Pack Track starts. After initially passing through forest, the trail opens out onto a section of rounded boulders beside the Fox River. Unless you want a 90-minute diversion up to the Fox River Cave (torches essential), cross the Fox River here to the true left. The track resumes on the far side, passing beneath layered limestone bluffs and through a mixture of podocarp–broadleaf forest where abundant nikau palms lend everything a subtropical look. Shortly before the junction with Dilemma Creek, cross the Fox River and head upstream for a further 30 minutes to reach the Ballroom Overhang. Despite its impressive size, the overhang is not drip-proof during wet weather, so take a tent.

Ballroom Overhang to Bullock Creek via Dilemma Creek 4–5 hours, 12 km

Head back down the Fox River to Dilemma Creek. Travel up the creek is generally untracked, involving multiple crossings, but trampers are rewarded with exquisitely mossy limestone formations set in a tight gorge. After a couple of hours, the narrow section of Dilemma Creek opens out, and

after a further 15 minutes or so the route turns up Fossil Creek (where camping is possible). Be careful to ensure you head up the right creek. After 30 minutes' travel in Fossil Creek, a marked track begins on the true left. In contrast to the river gorges, the next section of track passes through undulating forested terrain – a mixture of beech and stately podocarps – emerging after a couple of hours onto farmland at Bullock Creek. After crossing Bullock Creek, follow the large orange markers along a farm road until it rejoins the Inland Pack Track. (Bullock Creek Road leads out to State Highway 6 and is an alternative shortcut.) Soon afterwards, the track returns to the forest and heads southwards towards the Pororari River.

Bullock Creek to Punakaiki via Pororari River 3–3.5 hours, 8 km

The track reaches the Pororari River downstream of its junction with Cave Creek. Cross the river to the true left where the track turns downstream. The Pororari is similar but more subtle than the Fox River; while its limestone cliffs are not quite as precipitous, it's a distinctive Paparoa canyon nonetheless. A well-graded track follows the true left bank all the way to Punakaiki, the emerald-green waters of the Pororari in places having sculpted the limestone masterfully.

Ballroom Overhang
< Dilemma Ck
< Fossil Ck
< Bullock Ck
Fox River Caves
Cave Ck >
< Fox R.
< Punakaiki R.
Pororari R. >
Tiromoana
Bullock Creek Rd
6
6
NORTH
Perpendicular Pt
Punakaiki
Dolomite Pt
(Pancake Rocks)

PAPAROA RANGE

Pororari River

Grade Easy–medium

Maps Topo50 BS19 Punakaiki, BS20 Charleston.

Access Tiromoana/Fox River carpark is 13 km north of Punakaiki on State Highway 6 between Greymouth and Westport. The tramp requires a car juggle or using public transport.

Shelter The Ballroom Overhang is not drip-proof in wet weather, so take a tent.

Information DOC Paparoa National Park Visitor Centre, 4294 Coast Road, Punakaiki, tel: 03 731 1895, email: paparoavc@doc.govt.nz

ST JAMES WALKWAY
LEWIS PASS 4–6 DAYS

At 66 km, the St James Walkway is the most alpine of New Zealand's walkways, passing through mountainous terrain in the northern reaches of the Southern Alps. Work on the walkway and huts began in 1979, at the height of the walkways movement, and two years later the St James was officially opened. The track passes through land of varying tenure, ranging from Lewis Pass National Reserve, to Lake Sumner Forest Park and the St James Conservation Area – formerly New Zealand's largest high-country pastoral lease.

The route takes in a mixture of beech forests, open high-country flats and river valleys. None of the sections is particularly strenuous, and the two 'passes' the walk crosses are so gentle as to hardly deserve the name. However, much of the track is reasonably high, and the numerous open areas are exposed to bad weather. While the St James can be enjoyed in any season, most trampers tackle it in summer or autumn. During winter and spring, the views of the snow-capped Spenser Mountains are at their best, although heavy snowfalls could make sections hard-going. It's possible to walk it in either direction, although clockwise (described here) involves slightly less climbing.

Lewis Pass entrance to Cannibal Gorge Hut (20 bunks, woodburner) 3–3.5 hours, 7 km

From the tarns and wetlands at the Lewis Pass carpark, boardwalks lead to an intentions book and the start of the St James Walkway. The well-graded and well-benched track descends steadily into the Right Branch of the Maruia River, which is crossed on a substantial footbridge at the bottom of Cannibal Gorge – so named from a brutal clash between two rival Maori parties in pre-European times.

Beyond, the track sidles high above Cannibal Gorge, crossing many small side streams before emerging onto the clearing where Cannibal Gorge Hut sits. Be aware that marked sections of this track can be prone to avalanches, so in winter pass through them quickly without stopping.

Cannibal Gorge Hut to Ada Pass Hut (14 bunks, woodburner) 1.5 hours, 3 km

Beyond Cannibal Gorge Hut the track continues through beech forest, with occasional glimpses of the high Freyberg Range, until crossing a footbridge over the Maruia River shortly before Ada Pass Hut.

Ada Pass Hut to Christopher Hut (14 bunks, woodburner) 3.5–4.5 hours, 10.5 km

Beyond Ada Pass Hut a gentle ascent leads to the open tussock grassland of Ada Pass (1008 m). A gentle descent into the Ada Valley leads through more forest until views open out to the Spenser Mountains, a spectacular range at the southern end of Nelson Lakes National Park. Not far beyond the confluence of the Christopher and Ada rivers, you reach the Christopher (or Ada) Cullers Hut, a small four-bunker originally built for deer hunters. The larger Christopher Hut is 10–15 minutes further on, and offers the best views of any hut on the walkway.

Christopher Hut to Anne Hut (20 bunks, woodburner) 4–5 hours, 13.5 km

From Christopher Hut the walkway carves an arc around two impressive peaks with suitably lofty names, Mt Federation and Philosophers Knob, passing from the Ada River into the Henry River. Most of the day follows open grassy flats where once St James Station cattle and horses grazed, and a substantial part of the walkway here follows old vehicle

tracks. The Henry River is crossed via a footbridge about 90 minutes from Anne Hut.

Anne Hut to Boyle Flat Hut (12 bunks, woodburner) 7–8 hours, 17.5 km

This section of the walkway is the longest and most strenuous, with a mixture of beech forest and open grassy flats. From Anne Hut, the track traverses a terrace before descending to the Anne River, which is soon crossed on a footbridge to reach the historic Anne Cullers Hut (4 bunks). Sixty minutes beyond this hut, it crosses again to the true left, then begins a steady ascent towards Anne Saddle (1136 m), where there are excellent views of the nearby Libretto and Opera ranges. A steepish descent leads into the headwaters of the Boyle River, which is followed for the remainder of the day to Boyle Flat Hut, passing the historic three-bunk Rokeby Hut en route.

Boyle Flat Hut to Boyle Village 5 hours, 14.5 km

The final day of the walk passes largely through part of Lake Sumner Forest Park. From the hut you cross a footbridge to the true left of the Boyle River, which is followed as far as a signposted junction marking the track to Magdalen Hut (6 bunks, woodburner), which provides alternative accommodation 30 minutes off the main walkway. From the track junction, another footbridge leads across to the true right of the Boyle River, where the track remains until it reaches another swingbridge. Here, back on the true left, follow a vehicle track for 30 minutes to reach the Boyle Village Outdoor Education Centre, located a short distance from State Highway 7.

Above *Winter over Lewis Pass and Maruia Valley*

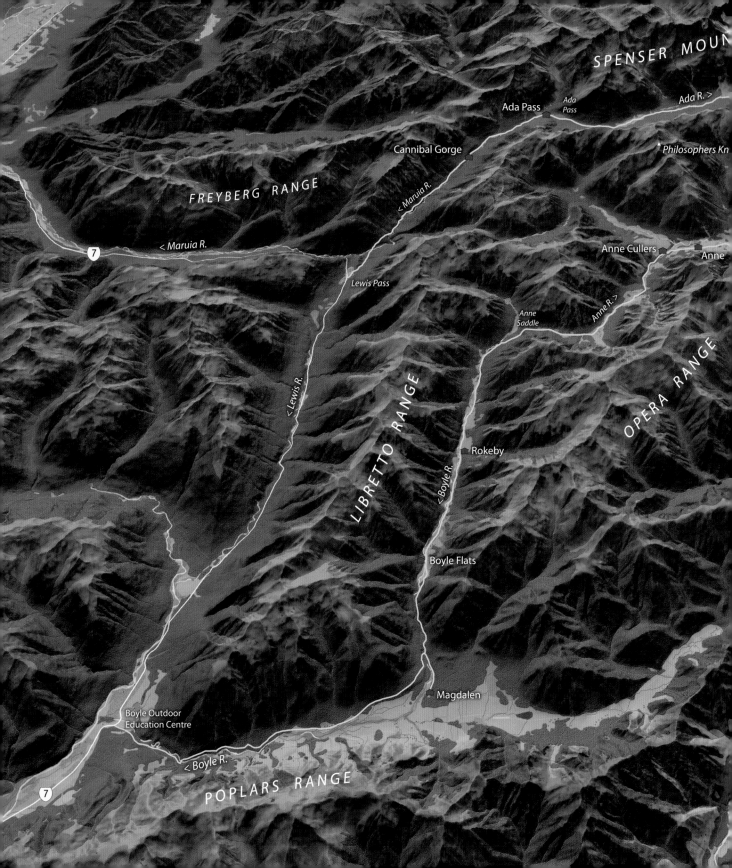

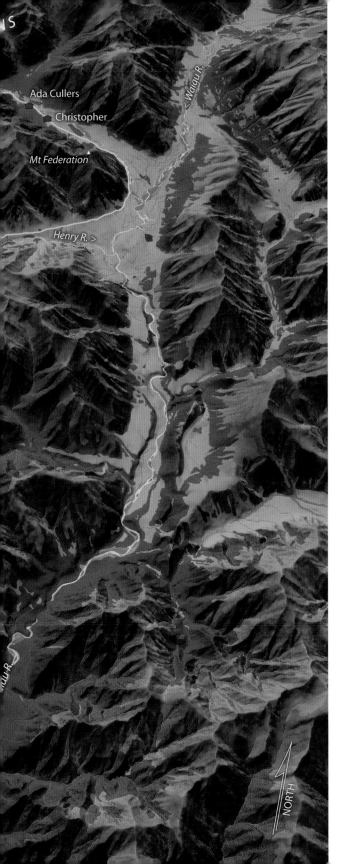

Ada Cullers

Christopher

Mt Federation

< Waiau R.

Henry R. >

NORTH

Grade Easy–medium

Maps Topo50 BT23 Lewis Pass, BT24 Ada Flat, BU23 Boyle Village

Access Situated near Lewis Pass on State Highway 7, the track begins from a carpark and picnic area 21 km from Springs Junction, or 228 km from Nelson and 187 km from Christchurch. The Boyle River entrance is 30 km south of Lewis Pass on the same highway, and is the safest place to leave your car. The Boyle River Outdoor Education Centre offers secure parking and a drop-off service for a moderate fee (tel: 03 315 7082). Alternatively, buses serve both entrances.

Huts All the large huts on the St James cost $15/night, or $7.50 for youths aged 11–17. Magdalen Hut costs $5/night, or $2.50 for youths. Christopher Cullers Hut, Anne Cullers Hut and Rokeby Hut are free. No booking is required for any of the huts.

Information DOC Waimakariri, 32 River Road, Rangiora, tel: 03 313 0820, email: waimakariri@doc.govt.nz

Maruia River, Cannibal Gorge

HARPER PASS
ARTHUR'S PASS NATIONAL PARK AND LAKE SUMNER FOREST PARK
4–6 DAYS

Few tramps in New Zealand are imbued with as much history as Harper Pass. To South Island Maori, the low saddle between the heads of the Hurunui and Taramakau rivers was one of the most important passages across the Southern Alps, over which pounamu (greenstone) could be transported from the West Coast. In 1857, Leonard Harper travelled over the old greenstone trail, becoming the first European to cross the South Island from coast to coast over the Southern Alps, and his name has been linked to the pass ever since. During the mid-1860s, Harper Pass enjoyed a brief period of popularity when gold prospectors rushed over to mine newly discovered goldfields on the West Coast, but the more direct route over Arthur's Pass soon eclipsed it.

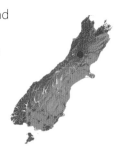

In the late 1930s, the government decided to reopen the track over Harper Pass, hoping to create a tramp that would rival the Milford Track. Although its scenery does not seriously rival that of Fiordland, the 77 km route offers an enjoyable and relatively easy way to cross the Southern Alps, connecting the Arthur's Pass and Lewis Pass highways. Attractive beech forests, several lakes, good birdlife, open river valleys, a generous number of huts and one hot spring all add to its appeal. Although the Canterbury side of the route is well tracked and bridged, some route-finding is required on the West Coast side. In addition, the Otira, Otehake and Taramakau rivers can all be impossible to negotiate after heavy rain.

Aickens to Locke Stream Hut (18 bunks, open fire) 6–8 hours, 18 km

At the carpark on State Highway 73 near Aickens, sign in at the intentions book. Poles lead across farmland to a ford at the Otira River. This is a serious ford, and should not be attempted if the river is high or discoloured. Alternatively, there is a flood route that uses a footbridge over the Otira south of Aickens, which avoids the ford but adds an extra two hours to the tramp.

The gravelly Taramakau River provides generally easy travel along a mixture of track through beech forest on river terraces and in the riverbed itself. At the Pfeifer Creek junction a side-track leads up to Lake Kaurapataka, a worthwhile diversion for those who have the time. From the lake it's possible to travel down the Otehake to join the main Taramakau Valley route (this will add 3–4 hours to the tramp).

Kiwi Hut (8 bunks, open fire), on the true right of the river, lies on a large bush terrace about 2 km upstream of the Otehake/Taramakau junction, and marks the halfway point to Locke Stream Hut. From here, trampers usually pick their own route up the valley, crossing the Taramakau River as required. Above Locke Stream, a track resumes on the true left and leads through bush for 15 minutes to reach the restored historic Locke Stream Hut, originally built in 1940.

Locke Stream Hut to Harper Pass Biv (2 bunks) via Harper Pass 3–3.5 hours, 7 km

Above Locke Stream, a well-marked track leads up the valley on the true left, crossing a footbridge to the true right after an hour or so. Travel steepens for the final section up to Harper Pass, which is awkward and rutted in places, but soon breaks out into subalpine shrublands. The 962 m pass,

View over Lake Sumner from Macs Knob

marked by a large sign, affords views of high mountains on both the Crawford and Kaimata ranges on either side. A track leads down into the headwaters of the Hurunui River, crossing to the true right shortly before reaching the small orange Harper Pass Biv.

Harper Pass Biv to Hurunui No. 3 Hut (16 bunks, woodburner) 3 hours, 9 km

From the biv, easy travel through increasingly attractive beech forests leads down old river terraces on the true right of the Hurunui. At Camerons Hut (4 bunks, open fire), the track emerges onto the first of many open grassy flats, which were grazed until recently. Downstream of Camerons Hut, the track crosses a three-wire bridge over Cameron Stream, followed by flat travel to Hurunui No. 3 Hut, set in a clearing. DOC has a locked research base nearby, which is used for undertaking pest control and wildlife work in the valley.

Hurunui No. 3 Hut to Hurunui Hut (15 bunks, woodburner) 3.5–4 hours, 10 km

The track continues eastwards, sidling through pleasant stands of beech forest above the Hurunui River, and pausing to divert to the Hurunui hot springs on a signposted side-track after about 90–120 minutes. These natural springs, perfect for a winter soak, offer room for about five to six people. About another 90–120 minutes of travel leads to the Hurunui Hut.

Hurunui Hut to Hope Kiwi Lodge (20 bunks, woodburner) 6 hours, 18 km

From Hurunui Hut it is possible to shorten the tramp by walking out to the Lake Taylor campsite and ending at the Lake Sumner Road (6 hours, 18 kilometres). But the more interesting walk continues down to the shores of Lake Sumner, crossing the Hurunui River on a long swingbridge en route.

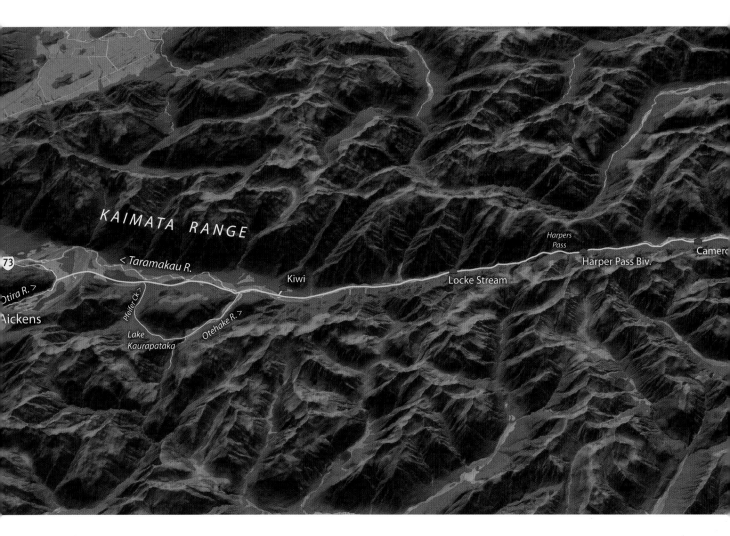

This section is known as the Hope Kiwi Track, or Kiwi Pack Track. It ambles over matagouri flats, then through stately red beech forests, and crosses a footbridge over the Three Mile Stream. Beyond, undulating forest travel on a beautifully benched track climbs steadily towards Kiwi Saddle. Near the track's high point, a two-minute side-track leads to a good viewpoint overlooking Lake Sumner. Another worthwhile side-track diverts to the tranquil Lake Marion. Beyond, the main track descends into the open, dell-like expanse of the Kiwi Valley. A retired farm vehicle track leads down the valley, through swampy flats, to the substantial and corralled Hope Kiwi Lodge.

Hope Kiwi Lodge to Windy Point via Hope Halfway Hut (6 bunks) 5–6 hours, 15 km

From the lodge, follow the track leading northwards to a swingbridge over the Hope River. From here, the landscape is basically a mixture of open river terraces and beech forest, with the track remaining on the true left of the Hope. Beyond Hope Halfway Hut (6 bunks), the track begins a slow climb onto river terraces high above the river. The last hour or so crosses scruffy farmland, descends to a swingbridge that spans a gorge in the Boyle River, then continues to the shelter at Windy Point.

THE NELSON TOPS

Hope R. >

Boyle R. >

Windy Point

Mackenzie Strm >

Three Mile Strm >

Hope Kiwi Lodge

Hope R. >

urunui No.3

Hurunui R. >

hot springs

Hurunui

Kiwi Saddle

Lake Marion

Hope Kiwi Track

Lake Sumner

CRAWFORD RANGE

Lake Katrine

Lake Mason

Hurunui R. Sth Branch >

Lake Shepherd

NORTH

Lake Taylor

Grade Medium

Maps Topo50 BU21 Haupiri, BU22 Lake Sumner, BU23 Boyle Village

Access The tramp starts at Aickens, State Highway 73, 78 km from Hokitika or 168 km from Christchurch. It ends at Windy Point on State Highway 7, 160 km from Christchurch. Buses and shuttles regularly service both routes.

Huts Hope Kiwi Lodge costs $15/night, or $7.50 for youths aged 11–17. Locke Stream, Hurunui No. 3 and Hurunui huts cost $5/night, or $2.50 for youths. Harper Pass Biv and Camerons Hut are free. No booking is required.

Information DOC Arthur's Pass Visitor Centre, State Highway 73, tel: 03 318 9211, email: arthurspassvc@doc.govt.nz DOC Waimakariri, 32 River Road, Rangiora, tel: 03 313 0820, email: waimakariri@doc.govt.nz

CASS–LAGOON SADDLE TRACK
CRAIGIEBURN FOREST PARK 2–3 DAYS

Because the Craigieburn Range lies on the drier eastern side of the main divide, it often provides a good tramping alternative when a nor'wester is drenching Arthur's Pass National Park. Although best known for its ski-fields, Canterbury's Craigieburn Forest Park offers good tramping, this walk being the most popular multi-day trip in the park. The 34 km track features one large hut and several smaller ones, two gentle passes, and pleasant valley walking. Although the track is not a circuit, it begins and ends on State Highway 73, where public transport is available. Although any season has its merits, during winter an amble over the Cass–Lagoon Saddle Track is often particularly rewarding, with the beech forests draped in snow. Be aware, however, that Cass Saddle can be prone to avalanches from Hamilton Peak. In summer, swimming in rivers offers a pleasant way to cool off when the weather proves hot.

State Highway 73 to Cass Saddle Hut (3 bunks, woodburner) 3.5–4 hours, 9 km

From the carpark, follow a vehicle track past a row of pine trees until it reaches the Cass River. Plod up the gravelly Cass River, at first staying mostly on the true left. The neat dip of Cass Saddle is visible ahead. Near the Long Valley Stream junction, a track begins on the true right, which sidles and climbs through beech forest. After an hour or so in the forest, cross a footbridge to the true left, where the track stays until shortly before Cass Saddle Hut.

Cass Saddle Hut to Hamilton Hut (20 bunks, woodburner) via Cass Saddle 2.5–3 hours, 8 km

Beyond the hut, the track soon breaks out of the bushline, where poles lead over the gentle Cass Saddle (1326 m). The saddle offers good views of the nearby Black Range and the Hamilton Valley – even as far as the hut. From Cass Saddle, the route drops almost immediately into beech forest, where a track leads down a steep escarpment to join Hamilton Creek. Once in the valley itself, the track remains on river terraces, crossing some matagouri-covered flats shortly before reaching the large and well-designed Hamilton Hut, with its sun-welcoming veranda. Good camping spots exist nearby.

For those with a day to spare, the 4–6-hour return trip to The Pinnacles is well worth the effort. Located in the lower Harper Valley, downstream of Hamilton Hut, these fantastically eroded pinnacles have resulted from the action of weathering on relatively young and soft rock, made from compressed gravels and sands. This side-trip requires crossing the Harper River, so should not be attempted if the river is high or if rain is due.

Hamilton Hut to Lagoon Saddle A-Frame Hut (2 bunks) 4–5 hours, 10 km

From Hamilton Hut, the track leads downstream to the junction with the Harper River. Two bridges are crossed in quick succession, the first (a three-wire) over Hamilton Creek and the second (a swingbridge) over the Harper. Between these bridges is a worthwhile side-track (20 minutes return) to Mirror Tarn, a small lake surrounded by forest.

Beyond the second bridge, the track remains on the true right of the Harper, sometimes in the bush and sometimes on gravelly river terraces. The West Harper Hut (a historic mustering shelter), with a dirt floor and canvas bunks, is not an attractive place to stay, but would suffice in an emergency. About a kilometre beyond the hut, the track climbs shortly and sharply over a low shoulder to avoid a

gorge in the river, then follows cairns along the riverbed for another kilometre or so. Past the Mangos Creek junction, be careful to pick up the track heading up the Harper (marked by a large orange triangle) and not accidentally head up the Long Creek tributary, which is as large as the Harper. The track remains on the true left until reaching the A-frame Lagoon Saddle Shelter. Another two-bunk hut occupies a position on the far bank, but has no windows or mattresses.

Lagoon Saddle A Frame Hut to State Highway 73 via Bealey Hut 2–3 hours, 7 km

From the shelter, the track ascends through thinning beech forest to emerge onto the flanks of Mt Bruce. After a short section of boardwalk, the route becomes poled, crossing a sometimes muddy section of track. Panoramic views over the mountains of the Waimakariri Basin unfold. After an hour or so along the tops, the track descends at a gentle gradient into pine forest, then beech forest, reaching Bealey Hut (6 bunks) just five minutes before the road end and car-park at Cora Lynn. A 10-minute walk along Cora Lynn Road leads to State Highway 73.

Grade Medium–hard
Maps Topo50 BV20 Otira, BV21 Cass, BW20 Lake Coleridge
Access The track begins near Cass on State Highway 73 (122 km from Christchurch) and ends at Cora Lynn, 12 km further on. Buses and shuttles service the route daily.
Huts Hamilton Hut costs $15/night, or $7.50 for youths aged 11–17. The remainder of the huts are free. No booking is required.
Information DOC Arthur's Pass Visitor Centre, State Highway 73, tel: 03 318 9211, email: arthurspassvc@doc.govt.nz DOC Waimakariri, 32 River Road, Rangiora, tel: 03 313 0820, email: waimakariri@doc.govt.nz

AVALANCHE PEAK
ARTHUR'S PASS NATIONAL PARK 2 DAYS

A traverse of Avalanche Peak to Crow Hut offers trampers a sample of the best alpine scenery in Arthur's Pass National Park. Over two days, trampers encounter terrain ranging from mountain beech forests to subalpine tussocklands, and alpine mountains to braided rivers, with superb vistas of the surrounding peaks, notably Mt Rolleston/Kaimatau.

In good summer and autumn conditions, trampers will encounter no undue difficulties following the poled route to the summit of Avalanche Peak. Beyond the peak, however, the rough route requires a good head for heights and the ability to negotiate loose scree. During winter and spring, trampers require mountaineering skills and equipment and should check avalanche conditions at the visitor centre before they leave. As the 18 km tramp involves a solid 1100 m vertical climb, parts of which are very exposed, undertake the trip only when the weather forecast is good.

Arthur's Pass Visitor Centre to Avalanche Peak
3.5–4 hours, 3.5 km

Two tracks lead through forest onto the lower flanks of Avalanche Peak. The slightly longer but gentler Scotts Track begins 700 m north of the visitor centre, opposite the Devils Punchbowl Track, and climbs steeply. Above the bushline, orange marker poles indicate the route up a tussock ridge.

The Avalanche Creek Track rises steeply from directly behind the visitor centre, climbing over sometimes rocky terrain with views of the nearby gorge and waterfall. Above the bushline it's marked by yellow poles, and climbs a tussock-covered ridge that narrows into a rocky spur.

Both routes join for the last narrow section of the summit ridge, culminating in Avalanche Peak (1833 m). Take care beside steep drop-offs. Mt Rolleston/Kaimatau lies barely 4 km away, as well as the myriad other peaks.

Avalanche Peak to Crow Hut (10 bunks, wood-burner) 2–3 hours, 3.5 km

From Avalanche Peak, a cairned route drops down onto the ridge leading towards Rolleston's pyramidal Low Peak. This section requires some negotiation, and is followed by a sidle across a face onto the broad ridge beyond.

To reach the Crow Valley, you must drop down a scree gully, just north of Pt 1658 m. Be very careful to ensure you reach the right gully (marked by a pole and cairn), as two false gullies (both encountered earlier along the ridge) end in impossible bluffs. From the top of the correct gully you should be able to see the entire scree slide right down to the floor of the Crow Valley, and in the other direction the entire 130 m drop of the Devils Punchbowl Falls.

Entering the steep gully requires care. During summer, it offers an exhilarating scree run, but in winter it may be icy or prone to avalanches. Once in the valley floor, head down the riverbed for a kilometre or so until you see Crow Hut perched on a terrace on the true right. The hut, opened in 2002, affords good views up-valley of the Crow Glacier.

Crow Hut to Klondyke Corner via Crow and Waimakariri Rivers 3–4 hours, 11 km

The walk out to the Waimakariri Valley is a pleasant amble beside the boisterous Crow River, initially on the true right, but crossing to the true left after two to three hours. Near the junction with the Waimakariri River, you cross a substantial forested river flat, then it's simply a matter of boulder-hopping down the riverbed to the camping area and road end near Klondyke Corner. Where the Waimakariri pushes in close to the beech forest, it's often simpler and faster to ford and then reford the river, providing conditions allow this.

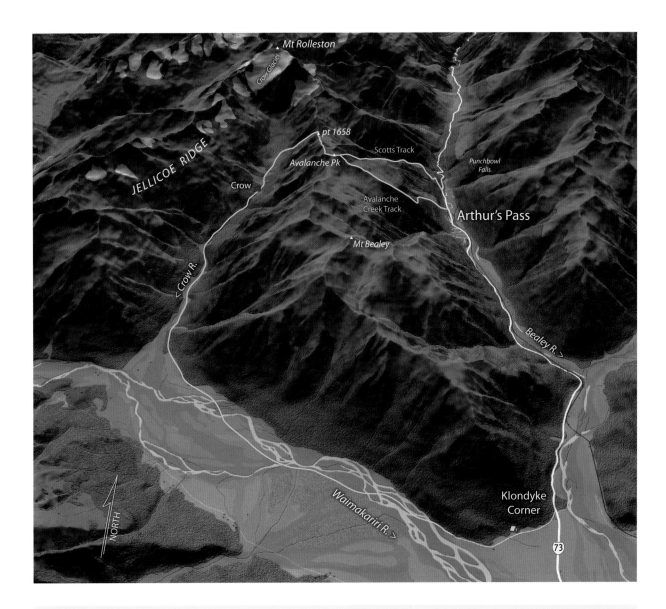

Grade Hard

Map Topo50 BV20 Otira

Access Arthur's Pass Village, on State Highway 73, is 140 km from Christchurch and 96 km from Greymouth. The track begins behind the carpark at the Arthur's Pass Visitor Centre, and ends at Klondyke Corner, both on State Highway 73 but 8 km apart. Buses and shuttles service the highway daily.

Hut Crow Hut costs $5/night, or $2.50 for youths aged 11–17. No booking is required.

Information DOC Arthur's Pass Visitor Centre, State Highway 73, tel: 03 318 9211, email: arthurspassvc@doc.govt.nz

CEDAR FLAT HUT
TOAROHA VALLEY, WEST COAST 2 DAYS

Diverse forests, impressive schist gorges and striking mountains all feature abundantly on the West Coast. Although the area is full of huts, many are rarely visited by trampers because of difficult access along tracks that are often slow-going through tortuous terrain. One exception is Cedar Flat Hut, reached via an accessible overnight tramp from the backblocks of Hokitika. The flats are reached on a good, largely benched track, which climbs around a formidable gorge in the Toaroha River known as the Toaroha Canyon. At Cedar Flat are two huts: a 12-bunk trampers' hut, and a historic two-bunk deer-cullers' hut (originally built in 1957, and recently restored). The distinctively conical pahautea, or mountain cedar, dominates the flats around the huts, set against a backdrop of the surrounding mountains. An added bonus is the nearby natural hot spring.

Upper Kokatahi Road to Cedar Flat Hut (12 bunks, woodburner) 4–5 hours, 10 km

From the road end, the track initially crosses farmland surrounding the Toaroha River, following the line of an old bush tramway, but soon enters the forest. Although well benched in places, part of the track through the forest has been rerouted to avoid slips, and climbs for 200 m. After

about 90 minutes, the track descends a steepish slip to emerge on the banks of the Toaroha.

Boulder-hop up the true right, past three side streams, to where the track resumes. Beyond, the track climbs steadily for 300 m to Petrologist Ridge, avoiding the Toaroha Canyon, which thunders ominously in the distance.

From the ridge, the track descends gently to flats, which are followed to a swingbridge over the Toaroha River. The Cedar Flat huts are located on the far bank.

The hot pools (marked on the topo map by a red cross) are a 15-minute walk from the hut: cross back over the swingbridge, walk 200 m up the Toaroha River, then head about 100 m up Wren Creek. While they can be unreliable, and may need digging out with the shovel provided, the hot pools make a pleasant place to ease aching muscles.

More experienced trampers may like to tackle day trips up to Yeats Ridge or Adventure Biv and onto the tops beyond. These are hard tramps, however, and should be undertaken only by those with sound navigation skills.

After a night or two at Cedar Flat, walk back out to the road end.

Left *Tramper crossing the Toaroha River* HUGH VAN NOORDEN
Opposite *Cedar Flat Hut* HUGH VAN NOORDEN

TOAROHA RANGE

DIEDRICHS RANGE

Adventure Biv.

Yeats Ridge

Wren Strm > hot springs

< Kokatahi R.

Petrologist Ridge

Cedar Flat

Toaroha Canyon

< Toaroha R.

Kokatahi
road end

NORTH

Grade Easy-medium

Map Topo 50 BV19 Lake Kaniere

Access From Hokitika, take the Kaniere Road to Kaniere (4 km), then turn off onto the Kaniere–Kowhitirangi Road and follow this for 10 km to reach Kokatahi. Here, take Middle Branch Road. The Toaroha Valley Road branches off left after a further 12 km.

Hut Cedar Flat Hut costs $5 for adults, or $2.50 for youths aged 11–17. No booking is required.

Information DOC Hokitika, 2 Sewell Street, Hokitika, tel: 03 756 9100, email: hokitika@doc.govt.nz

WELCOME FLAT
WESTLAND TAI POUTINI NATIONAL PARK 2–5 DAYS

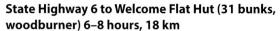

The Copland Pass track dates back to the nineteenth century, when it was a popular route linking the Hermitage at Mount Cook with the hotels near the West Coast glaciers. Recently, however, glacial recession in the Hooker Valley has made the crossing beyond the skill of most trampers. Though, fortunately, trampers can still enjoy the tracks in the Copland Valley.

Welcome Flat Hut is located near some of the country's finest hot pools, where trampers can gaze languorously onto the Sierra Range. Past Welcome Flat, the track continues to Douglas Rock Hut. Beyond, experienced trampers can explore the valley head as far as Fitzgerald Pass (which from the west has an easier approach than the more precipitous Copland Pass). The Pass offers stupendous views of the highest peaks in the Southern Alps, and during early summer the valley head abounds with flowering alpine plants.

State Highway 6 to Welcome Flat Hut (31 bunks, woodburner) 6–8 hours, 18 km

The Copland Track starts just north of the road bridge over the Karangarua River. The track heads immediately up the valley, on the true right of the Karangarua, soon reaching Rough Creek. While there is a flood route to a footbridge located about 1.5 km upstream, Rough Creek provides an excellent gauge of river levels. If you can ford it easily, the chances are none of the streams up the valley will cause problems. However, if Rough Creek is high or discoloured, it's wise to turn back.

Beyond, the track crosses flat terrain to reach the Copland Valley, where the track narrows noticeably. It passes through forest, emerging only where it crosses numerous side creeks. Most of these are bridged, although others can cause problems after heavy rain. About halfway to Welcome Flat, Architect Creek Hut (2 bunks, woodburner) offers respite from the sandflies. Beyond Open Creek, the climbing becomes more noticeable, and the track crosses a couple of active slips, which can be unstable after heavy rain.

The popular Welcome Flat Hut must be booked in advance, but a nearby rock biv provides further accommodation. The hot pools lie five minutes away, where views of the Sierra Range can be enjoyed at a perfect soaking temperature. Because of the risk of contracting amoebic meningoencephalitis, don't submerge your head.

Welcome Flat Hut to Douglas Rock Hut (8 bunks, woodburner) 4–5 hours, 8 km

Only experienced trampers should proceed beyond Welcome Flat. Shortly past the hut, the track crosses a footbridge to the true left of the Copland River, where it remains for the rest of the tramp. Initially, the track crosses the extensive Welcome Flat. Scott Creek, near the end of the flat, can flood quickly after rain. Beyond Scott Creek, the track begins an ascent to Douglas Rock Hut, situated in the last copse of trees in the valley.

Douglas Rock Hut to Fitzgerald Pass 7–10 hours return, 7.5 km each way

Only attempt this route if you have alpine skills (take an ice axe and crampons) It involves a 1400 m ascent, and can be subject to avalanches.

Upstream of Douglas Rock Hut the route climbs above the last of the subalpine shrubs, with expansive views opening out. Mt Sefton rears impressively to the south, while Dilemma and Unicorn peaks dominate the northern view. The track, marked by cairns and poles, sidles about 100 m above the Copland River until directly below Copland Pass, where it zigzags up beside bluffs into an alpine basin. Beyond, easier slopes lead towards the crest of the Southern Alps. The 2150 m Copland Pass is the less obvious pass on the left; Fitzgerald Pass (2109 m) lies to the right.

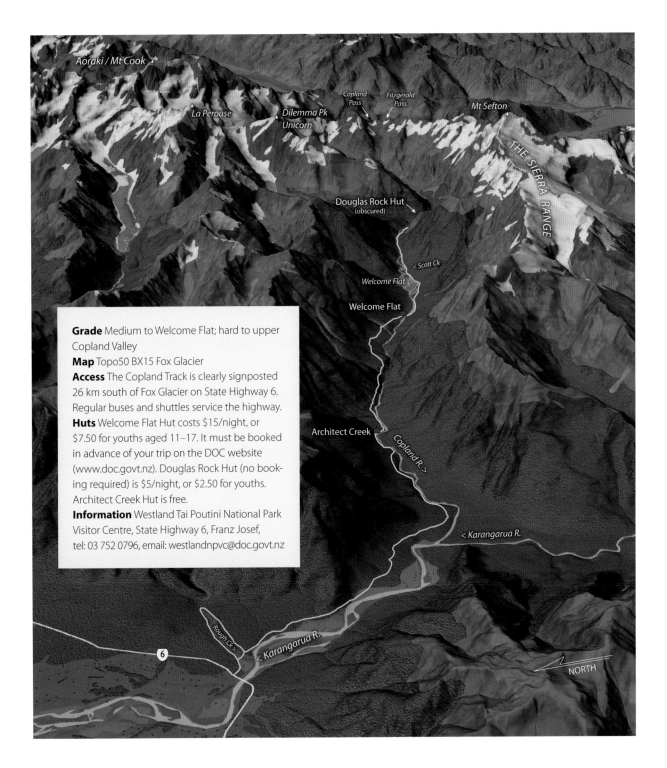

Aoraki / Mt Cook

La Perouse

Dilemma Pk
Unicorn

Copland
Pass

Fitzgerald
Pass

Mt Sefton

THE SIERRA RANGE

Douglas Rock Hut
(obscured)

< Scott Ck

Welcome Flat

Welcome Flat

Grade Medium to Welcome Flat; hard to upper
Copland Valley
Map Topo50 BX15 Fox Glacier
Access The Copland Track is clearly signposted
26 km south of Fox Glacier on State Highway 6.
Regular buses and shuttles service the highway.
Huts Welcome Flat Hut costs $15/night, or
$7.50 for youths aged 11–17. It must be booked
in advance of your trip on the DOC website
(www.doc.govt.nz). Douglas Rock Hut (no book-
ing required) is $5/night, or $2.50 for youths.
Architect Creek Hut is free.
Information Westland Tai Poutini National Park
Visitor Centre, State Highway 6, Franz Josef,
tel: 03 752 0796, email: westlandnpvc@doc.govt.nz

Architect Creek

Copland R. >

< Karangarua R.

6

Rough Ck >

< Karangarua R.

NORTH

MUELLER HUT
AORAKI/MOUNT COOK NATIONAL PARK 2 DAYS

Mueller Hut is undoubtedly one of the best-located alpine tramping huts in New Zealand. Perched high on the Sealy Range, the large, modern hut overlooks not only the towering pyramid of Aoraki/ Mt Cook, but the even more dramatic, avalanche-prone eastern ice cliffs of Mt Sefton. A climb to the hut offers one of the few opportunities for trampers to get among the peaks of Aoraki/ Mount Cook National Park, normally a domain for mountaineers.

While reasonably straightforward, this alpine tramp is a strenuous one, suitable only for experienced trampers. When snow lies on the route, trampers will need an ice axe and crampons, and the ability to use them. In total, reaching Mueller Hut entails a 1000 m climb, and can be prone to avalanches at any time of year, so check with DOC before you set off. The current Mueller Hut, completed in 2003, can accommodate 28 people, and is the fifth hut to occupy the area. It must be booked in advance of your tramp.

Aoraki/Mount Cook Village to Mueller Hut
(28 bunks, gas cookers) 4–5 hours, 5.2 km

From Aoraki/Mount Cook Village, follow the Kea Point Track northwards. A short distance past White Horse Hill, branch off on the Sealy Tarns track. Here, on a steep 400 m

climb, with many sets of stairs, you pass through subalpine shrublands and herbfields to emerge onto the rocky tussock tops. The Sealy Tarns are attractive small alpine lakes that, on a fine day, offer superb views and reflections of Aoraki/Mt Cook. Beyond Sealy Tarns, the alpine route is marked by cairns. After crossing tussock slopes and a boulder field, trampers climb up a steep scree slope to gain the prominent spur at the end of the Sealy Range.

From here, the climbing eases, weaving a route between boulders up the ridge to Mueller Hut. Surrounded by some of the highest and most glaciated mountains in New Zealand, Mueller is a superbly situated alpine hut, where many hours can be spent watching the ice cliffs of Mt Sefton crumble onto the Mueller Glacier below.

Mt Ollivier (1933 m), the first peak climbed by Sir Edmund Hillary (who was later the first to ascend Mt Everest with Tenzing Norgay), is a rock scramble about a kilometre from the hut. From the summit, the prominent ridge visible on Aoraki/Mt Cook is suitably called the Hillary Ridge. Beyond Mt Ollivier, only those with mountaineering equipment and experience should tackle travel on the Sealy Range.

Left Dawn over Mueller Hut and Mt Sefton
Opposite Sunrise on Mt Sefton from the Sealy Range

Grade Medium–hard

Map Topo50 BX15 Fox Glacier

Access Aoraki/Mt Cook Village is 330 km from Christchurch and 320 km from Dunedin. The excellent Aoraki/Mt Cook Visitor Centre has information on the park, weather and avalanche conditions, and an intentions book. Access to the tramp is on the Kea Point Track, beginning either from the village or from the White Horse Hill camping area.

Hut Mueller Hut costs $36/night, or $18 for youths aged 11–17. During the summer season (November to April) it must be booked in advance of your trip on the DOC website (www.doc.govt.nz).

Information Aoraki/Mt Cook Visitor Centre, Larch Grove, Mt Cook Village, tel: 03 435 1186, email: mtcookvc@doc.govt.nz

YOUNG–WILKIN TRACK
MT ASPIRING NATIONAL PARK 3–5 DAYS

Over recent years, increasing numbers of people have discovered this delightful round trip. The tramp crosses the alpine Gillespie Pass, linking the Young and Wilkin, two of the more accessible valleys in the northern part of Mt Aspiring National Park. While the 53-km track could be completed in as little as three days, those allowing another day or two can enjoy a side-trip to the exquisite Crucible Lake alpine tarn.

In summer, you'll be sharing the Siberia Valley with day walkers who fly in via fixed-wing aircraft, then walk out to a jet-boat pick-up near Kerin Forks. Independent tramp-ers can also arrange plane or jet-boat transport to shorten the trip, but must book this in advance.

Blue Pools carpark, State Highway 6, to Young River confluence, 1.5–2 hours, 7 km

Access to the Young–Wilkin Track begins 3 km north of Ma-karora on State Highway 6. The most direct route onto the track is to follow marker poles over farmland and then cross the Makarora River just north of its junction with the Young. However, crossing the Makarora should not be attempted in anything other than low to normal flow; if you have any doubts about river levels, it is safer to begin the tramp at the Blue Pools carpark, a further 5 km north on State High-way 6. Here, take the path to the Blue Pools, which crosses the Makarora River, then the Blue River, on substantial foot-bridges. Beyond the Blue Pools, the Blue–Young Link Track leads through beech forest on the true right of the river to reach the Young and Makarora confluence.

Young River confluence to Young Hut (20 bunks, woodburner) 6–7 hours, 20 km

Travel up the Young largely involves a gradual ascent through beech forest and mountain ribbonwood. At Young Forks, the river divides into the North and South branches. A few hundred metres up the North Branch is a shelter and formal campsite, and also a swingbridge across the river. If river levels are low, however, cross at the forks, and take the track up the South Branch towards Young Hut.

The next section of the track begins with a steady climb, sidling high above the boisterous waters of the Young River South Branch. Fortunate trampers might encounter flocks of the rare mohua (yellowhead) in the forest here. Young Hut sits on a flat terrace in the forest.

Young Hut to Siberia Hut (20 bunks, woodburner) via Gillespie Pass 6–8 hours, 12 km

Beyond Young Hut, the track emerges above the bushline after about 30 minutes. A poled route leads up into the Young Basin, a dramatic cirque beneath the imposing bluffs of Mt Awful. About a kilometre above the hut, the route be-gins an abrupt climb up a steep spur towards Gillespie Pass (note that the route crests the ridge at Pt 1574 m, not at Gillespie Pass itself). From the ridge crest, Mt Awful domi-nates, with the peaks of the main divide beyond.

The descent into Gillespie Stream begins steeply, but eases off lower down. After another steep section through subalpine scrub, you reach the stream, where there is a good place to camp. From here, the track sidles along the stream, climbs over a forested knoll, then begins a sharp de-scent down into the Siberia Valley. Siberia Hut lies a further hour downstream.

Opposite *Crossing Gillespie Pass, with Mt Awful beyond*

Side-trip to Crucible Lake
5–6 hours return, 3.5 km each way

From Siberia Hut, a steep but worthwhile side-trip takes you to a large alpine tarn called Crucible Lake. The track begins up the valley from Siberia Hut, near the Gillespie Stream and Siberia River confluence. From there, head up the Siberia Valley, cross the river where convenient, and pick up the track that begins beside the stream draining Crucible Lake. After a very steep climb, the route crosses the stream and sidles over tussock slopes towards the obvious large moraine at the valley head. From the top of the moraine wall, the turquoise-coloured Crucible Lake appears almost perfectly round. Small icebergs that have dislodged from the glacier of Mt Alba sometimes float on the lake.

Siberia Hut to Kerin Forks Hut (10 bunks, wood-burner) 3–4 hours, 11 km

The Siberia is a classic U-shaped valley, with the polished rock faces of Mt Dreadful at its head. On fine days such grand scenery is marred only by the buzz of small planes, depositing tourists on the nearby airstrip. During summer you'll likely meet some of these people walking out to the Wilkin River, from where they jet-boat down to Makarora. On the well-graded and well-benched track, it's a slow climb up above a gorge in the lower Siberia, then a steady descent through beech forest to the Wilkin River.

Many trampers choose to prearrange a jet-boat ride down the Wilkin River from Kerin Forks to Makarora. It's an exhilarating – if costly – way to end the trip, and saves having to cross either the Wilkin or Makarora rivers.

NORTH

Blue Pools carpark

Blue - Young
Link Track

6

Young R. >

Young R. Nth Branch >

Young
North Branch

Young R. Sth Branch >

Mt Awful

Young

Gillespie
Pass

Mt Turner

Gillespie Strm >

Siberia

Mt Dreadful

Siberia Strm >

Crucible Lake

Kerin For

Mt Alba

Siberia Strm >

< Wilkin R.

Makarora

Makarora R.

Wilkin R.

Dans Flat

Trampers who plan to spend a night at Kerin Forks Hut need to cross the river, which can be troublesome in all but the lowest river levels. The hut, not visible from the river, is set on a grassy slope about 400 m below the forks.

Kerin Forks Hut to Makarora via Wilkin River
4–5 hours, 15 km

Travel down the Wilkin Valley resumes on the true left, and consists of a mixture of beech forest and river flats, with cattle grazing the lower areas. Below Dans Flat, it may be quicker to cross the Wilkin to flats on the far side, then re-cross it at its confluence with the Makarora.

Grade Medium–hard
Map Topo50 BZ12 Makarora
Access Makarora township is located 63 km north of Wanaka on State Highway 6. It has a shop, café, accommodation and jet-boat services. The Blue Pools Walk starts 8 km north of Makarora.
Huts All three huts cost $15/night, or $7.50 for youths aged 11–17. No booking is required.
Information Tititea/Mt Aspiring National Park Visitor Centre, Ardmore Street, Wanaka, tel: 03 443 7660, email: wanakavc@doc.govt.nz

Young Hut

REES–DART TRACK
MT ASPIRING NATIONAL PARK 4–5 DAYS

The 63-km Rees–Dart Track links two of the most scenic valleys in Mt Aspiring National Park, with the option of a side-trip to Cascade Saddle, which is arguably one of the most spectacular locations in the Southern Alps. Essentially, the tramp circumnavigates Mt Earnslaw/Pikirakatahi (2830 m), a prominent glacier-covered mountain – the second highest in Mt Aspiring National Park.

In 2014, large landslides dammed the Dart River, and subsequently a sizeable lake formed that now occupies the valley floor for 3 km at Dredge Flat. This has inundated sections of the track, and also altered the course of the Dart River below the lake, obliterating more sections of the track. Despite efforts by DOC to reinstate a temporary route, one section between Chinamans Bluff and Bedford Stream is now impassable. Until DOC can reroute this section, trampers are advised to avoid it.

Instead, DOC recommends trampers walk up the Rees Valley to Dart Hut, where they can enjoy a side-trip to Cascade Saddle. Instead of walking down the Dart, trampers should retrace their route back into the Rees to end back at the carpark. Descriptions of the sections in the Dart Valley have been retained here, in anticipation that DOC will be able to reroute the track above the flooded section. Suitably experienced trampers can descend to the West Matukituki Valley from Cascade Saddle, but be aware this is a very steep and potentially treacherous descent. Trampers have died from falling here, and it is to be avoided when the route is wet or snow-covered.

Highlights of the Rees–Dart Track include views of Mt Earnslaw/Pikirakatahi, Rees Saddle, the Dart Glacier and Mt Aspiring/Tititea.

Rees Valley road end to Shelter Rock Hut (22 bunks, woodburner) 6–7 hours, 19 km

From the Muddy Creek carpark, follow a vehicle track across farmland. Beyond Arthurs Creek, a poled track leads to Twenty Five Mile Hut (8 bunks, open fire), owned by Rees Valley Station and maintained by the Otago Tramping and Mountaineering Club. Mt Earnslaw/Pikirakatahi dominates the views, with waterfalls spilling off its glaciated flanks.

Another couple of hours' easy walk leads to the end of the farmland, and the Mt Aspiring National Park boundary. Soon after entering the forest, the track crosses a footbridge leading to the true right of the Rees River.

Aside from one section of travel across Slip Flat, the remaining three hours' walk to Shelter Rock Hut remains largely within the confines of the forest. A kilometre or so from the hut, the forest gives way to subalpine shrublands. Just before Shelter Rock the track crosses the Rees again, on a footbridge.

Shelter Rock Hut to Dart Hut (30 bunks, woodburner) via Rees Saddle 4–6 hours, 10 km

Travel from Shelter Rock Hut to Dart Hut involves crossing the Rees Saddle (1471 m) at the head of the Rees. Although the route is well poled and normally straightforward, be aware that there are steep drop-offs in places, and under adverse weather conditions or heavy snow it may prove impassable. In winter, it is subject to avalanches.

Upstream of Shelter Rock Hut, a benched trail cuts through subalpine plants for an hour or so before breaking out into a tussock basin. Rees Saddle is the obvious

low point at the valley head. After crossing the river, poles lead up a steepish last pinch beneath impressive bluffs to the saddle. Here, a whole new vista opens out. Below lies Snowy Creek, with Mt Tyndall at its head – wide-open, mountainous country that typifies the Mt Aspiring National Park region.

After an initially steep descent, the track beside Snowy Creek levels out. About halfway down the valley, the track crosses a swingbridge (removed during winter months to avoid avalanche damage) to the true right. After another section of steep downhill, the track levels out again to cross the Snowy Creek on a footbridge shortly before Dart Hut.

Trampers descend toward Dart Glacier from Cascade Saddle

Side-trip to Cascade Saddle
8–10 hours return, 10 km each way

This side-trip is a strenuous and long day from Dart Hut, but well worth it for the exceptional views. It is not a formed track, so should be attempted only by those confident to navigate the poled and cairned route.

From Dart Hut, recross the footbridge over Snowy Creek and follow the poles and cairns into the upper Dart Valley. Further up, the route crosses the first of a series of moraine terraces left after the retreat of the once-extensive Dart

Trampers, Daleys Flat, Dart Valley, with Barrier Range beyond

Glacier. Two tributaries here could pose problems when in flood. After about three hours, the route begins to climb moraine and tussock slopes towards Cascade Saddle. There are increasingly good views of the Dart Glacier and Snow-drift Range. Cascade Saddle, situated on a large tussock shelf, offers unsurpassed views of Mt Aspiring/Tititea and the West Matukituki Valley. In summer, alpine flowers proliferate among the sheltered tarns and hollows of the saddle. Return to Dart Hut along the same route.

Dart Hut to Daleys Flat Hut (32 bunks, wood-burner) 5–7 hours, 18 km

The track down the valley from Dart Hut is long but not particularly strenuous, and initially sidles above the Dart River on the true left. Beech forest dominates until you reach Cattle Flat, a long 4 km grassy section marked by poles. There is a good rock bivouac on the edge of Cattle Flat, which offers a dry place to sleep, but it is exposed to sandflies! From Cattle Flat, travel on a good track leads through beech forest to Daleys Flat Hut.

Daleys Flat Hut to Chinamans Bluff carpark 8 hours, 16 km

From Daleys Flat Hut, a gentle track through beech forest leads to Dredge Flat. A new temporary route traverses the edge of the lake, meeting the old track at the base of Sandy Bluff. A stiff climb over Sandy Bluff ensues, offering some good views of the new lake in places. The stretch between Sandy Bluff and Bedford Stream is the section that has been inundated by the altered course of the Dart River, and is presently impassable.

Beyond Bedford Stream, the original well-graded and well-benched track resumes, and makes pleasant if sometimes monotonous walking, alternating between grassy flats and sections of stately beech forest. At Chinamans Bluff, there is a shelter, toilets and a carpark, which is accessible by two-wheel drives except after rain or snow. It's another 6 km to the all-weather carpark at Paradise.

Grade Medium–hard

Maps Topo50 CB10 Glenorchy, CA10 Lake Williamson, CA11 Aspiring Flats

Access Glenorchy is 46 km from Queenstown, and has accommodation, cafés, and shuttles that service both road ends. From Glenorchy, follow the Rees Valley Road for 22 km to the carpark at Muddy Creek. The tramp ends at the Paradise carpark on the Glenorchy–Paradise Road, 30 km from Glenorchy. Both access roads have gravelled sections and fords that may be impassable after rain.

Huts All huts on the Rees–Dart Track cost $15/night, or $7.50 for youths aged 11–17. No booking is required.

Information Whakatipu-wai-Maori/Queenstown Visitor Centre, 50 Stanley Street, Queenstown, tel: 03 442 7935, email: queenstownvc@doc.govt.nz

Mt Aspiring / Tititea

Dart
Glacier

SNOWDRIFT RANGE

Cascade
Saddle

West Matukituki R. >

Dart

Mt Tyndall

BARRIER RANGE

Cattle Flat

Rees Saddle → < Snowy Ck

Daleys Flat

Shelter Rock

FORBES MOUNTAINS

Dredge Flat

new lake
Jan 2014

Slip Flat

Sandy Bluff

Mt Earnslaw / Pikirakatahi

< Bedford Srm

FORBES MOUNTAINS

Twenty Five Mile

Chinamans Bluff

< Muddy Ck

Dart road end

Rees road end

Paradise

NORTH

< Dart R. / Te Awa Whakatipu

< Rees R.

GREENSTONE–CAPLES CIRCUIT
OTAGO 4 DAYS

This delightful track follows two large, open, glacier-carved valleys – the Caples and Greenstone – among stately beech forest, with grand peaks on either side. Both valleys boast flat and easy tracks, linked by the more strenuous but not difficult climb over McKellar Saddle. The Greenstone Valley once formed an important route from Lake Wakatipu for Maori to access pounamu in northern Fiordland, and in more recent times was part of the historical cattle route from Martins Bay.

It's not a pristine area; trampers share both valleys with sheep and cattle, run by farmers managing the land on behalf of Ngai Tahu, who own the valley floors. McKellar Saddle and the upper Greenstone Valley have the curious distinction of being the only part of Fiordland National Park in Otago.

With large, comfortable huts, and accessible in all seasons, the 61 km track makes a good introduction for novice trampers or adventurous family groups wanting to tackle a multi-day trip. The track can be walked in either direction. On the Greenstone Track a private company runs guided walks using private lodges, but only the independent option is described here.

Road end to Mid Caples Hut (24 bunks, wood-burner) 2–3 hours, 9 km

From the shelter at the road end, the well-benched track follows a stock race beside the emerald-green waters of the Greenstone River. Pass a large stock footbridge (where a side-track leads to Lake Rere) and continue up the valley, climbing gradually above a deep gorge. After 30 minutes, the track reaches a swingbridge over the Caples River. Bypass this and continue up the Caples Track, with Tooth Peak prominent.

The track remains on the true left among red beech forest until it crosses a spectacular narrow chasm on a footbridge just before Mid Caples Hut. Lying on a terrace on the true right, the hut offers good views of the Humboldt Mountains.

Mid Caples Hut to McKellar Hut (24 bunks, wood-burner) via McKellar Saddle 6–7 hours, 22 km

From Mid Caples Hut, the Caples Track heads up the valley on the true right, crossing grassy farm flats that can be muddy in winter. Further up, the track once again enters beech forest, passing some delightfully golden flats en route. Note that the Upper Caples Hut is now managed by the New Zealand Deerstalkers' Association (who also manage the Mid Greenstone Hut) and must be booked through them.

The track has been extensively upgraded in recent years, making the tramp over the McKellar Saddle much easier than it used to be, although it can still become impassable after heavy rain floods side creeks. Initially, the track from Upper Caples Hut crosses through beech forest on flat terraces, passing a swingbridge that leads to side-tracks up Kay and Fraser creeks. Soon after, it begins a gradual climb beside the upper Caples River. Above the bushline, McKellar Saddle (945 m) offers fine views of both the Caples and Greenstone valleys, with the Livingstone Mountains beyond. Mt Christina, in the Darran Mountains, rises prominently too. Boardwalks lead past fragile alpine tarns to where the track begins a 360 m descent into the Greenstone Valley. The rerouted track zigzags downwards through the beech forest, with occasional glimpses of Lake McKellar. Near the valley floor, the track detours up

Trampers crossing McKellar Saddle

the valley, then crosses the infant Greenstone River on a footbridge. On the far side, a signposted junction marks the connection with the Greenstone Track. Head down the valley towards Lake McKellar, a beech-fringed lake of considerable size. The Greenstone Track sidles through pleasant forest above the lake before reaching McKellar Hut. The hut occupies a clearing with views of the craggy Jean Batten Peak (1971 m).

McKellar Hut to Greenstone Hut (20 bunks, wood-burner) 4.5–6.5 hours, 18 km

Beyond McKellar Hut, the Greenstone Track crosses a swingbridge over the Greenstone River, and continues down the valley on its true left. The track stays largely in the forest, but often sidles along the edge of some large

tussock flats. In sunny weather, this section is a delight, with good views of the Livingstone Mountains and the sparkling waters of the Greenstone.

About three hours from McKellar Hut, the track crosses Steele Creek on a swingbridge, and soon afterwards passes Mid Greenstone Hut (managed by the New Zealand Deerstalkers' Association). Past the hut, an easy 90 minutes' travel leads down the rapidly growing Greenstone River. Greenstone Hut is reached via a signposted 10-minute side-track, which crosses a chasm in the Greenstone River on a footbridge. The hut occupies a sunny clearing with excellent views both up and down the valley.

Fraser Ck >

< Kay Ck

HUMBOLDT MO

Jean Batten Pk

Upper Caples

McKellar Saddle

Caples R. >

Lake McKellar

Mid Caples

McKellar

AILSA MOUNTAINS

LIVINGSTONE MOUNTAINS

Steele Ck >

Slip Strm >

Slip Flat Hu

Mid Greenstone

Greenstone R. >

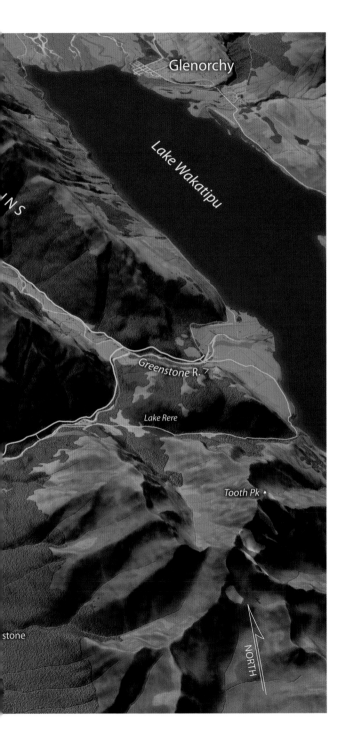

Greenstone Hut to Greenstone road end
3–5 hours, 12 km

From the hut, cross back to the true left and continue down the valley on a wide, benched track. After an hour or so the track crosses a footbridge over Slip Stream. Hut enthusiasts might be interested to locate Slip Flat Hut (3 bunks, open fire), an old character hut that lies 200–300 m off the track shortly beyond the footbridge. The main Greenstone Track continues down the valley, passing two narrow but high waterfalls en route and another side-track to Lake Rere. The valley narrows, with views of the distant Richardson Mountains (on the far side of Lake Wakatipu) shortly before emerging onto flats at the junction of the Greenstone and Caples. Cross the swingbridge over the Caples. The last leg of the walk is a reverse of the first 30 minutes of the first day, leading back to the carpark.

Grade Easy–medium

Maps Topo50 CB10 Glenorchy, CB09 Hollyford

Access Glenorchy is 46 km from Queenstown, and has accommodation and cafés. The track begins from the Greenstone road end, 40 km from Glenorchy and reached by driving through Kinloch. The last section of road is gravel with a couple of fords that may be impassable after rain. At the road end is a shelter and toilets. During the peak summer season, shuttles service the track from Glenorchy.

Huts and camping Mid Caples, McKellar and Greenstone huts cost $15/night, or $7.50 for youths aged 11–17. Slip Creek Hut is free. No booking is required. Please note that camping is not permitted on the privately owned Caples and Greenstone valley floors, nor on the fragile McKellar Saddle. Camping is allowed near the huts. The New Zealand Deerstalkers' Association manage both the Upper Caples and Mid Greenstone huts; both are locked and must be pre-booked (email: info@southernlakesnzda.org.nz).

Information Whakatipu-wai-Maori/Queenstown Visitor Centre, 50 Stanley Street, Queenstown, tel: 03 442 7935, email: queenstownvc@doc.govt.nz

ROUTEBURN TRACK
MT ASPIRING AND FIORDLAND NATIONAL PARKS 2–3 DAYS

The Routeburn is perhaps the most famous of New Zealand's tracks after the Milford. It connects the Dart Valley in Mt Aspiring National Park with the Hollyford Valley in Fiordland National Park, crossing landscapes of such diversity and splendour that you'd be hard pressed to find a better walk in the world.

From Tolkienesque beech forests to alpine lakes, waterfalls and mountain vistas, the 32 km Routeburn offers a concentration of the best South Island scenery. Indeed, so many have discovered the track's delights that a booking system is now in place for the peak summer season. During winter, it becomes the domain of experienced mountaineers only, as much of the tops section becomes prone to avalanches. A guided walk, using private huts, is also an option.

Routeburn Shelter to Routeburn Falls Hut (48 bunks, woodburner) via Routeburn Flats Hut
3.5–4 hours, 8.8 km

Beginning from the carpark near Routeburn Shelter, the well-benched and gravelled track soon crosses the Route Burn on a large footbridge. A slow climb ensues, on the true left of the Route Burn, past a schist-choked gorge through which the blue-green waters of the river tumble. Another footbridge leads back to the true right about 25 minutes before Routeburn Flats Hut (20 bunks, woodburner). The hut occupies the edge of an expansive tussock flat. While some trampers spend a night here, most parties push on along the Route Burn Left Branch to Routeburn Falls. Despite the substantial 300 m climb, the extremely well-graded track ensures the effort is hardly noticeable. The track crosses two footbridges en route, with the Emily Creek bridge considered to be about halfway.

While the large Routeburn Falls Hut has bunkrooms reminiscent of army barracks, its grand location provides adequate compensation. It is also well positioned to begin the next day's tramp over Harris Saddle.

Routeburn Falls Hut to Lake Mackenzie Hut (50 bunks, woodburner) via Harris Saddle
4.5–6 hours, 11.3 km

Above Routeburn Falls, the Route Burn once again becomes sedate, curling through boggy subalpine flats. Above, the track takes on a suitably alpine nature, passing through tussock grasslands and herbfields. Higher up, the track curls up over moraines and across cliffs above Lake Harris. The lake, which occupies a glacier-carved basin of textbook precision, is the source of Route Burn and is itself fed by numerous cascades. Past the narrow sidle through bluffs, the track bends around a shoulder and over the broad Harris Saddle. Here, you enter Fiordland National Park and reach the basic Harris Saddle Shelter (day use only). A steep 260 m side-trip leads to Conical Hill (1515 m), one of the best viewpoints on the tramp.

The next section of the track skirts the avalanche-prone Hollyford Faces, with excellent views of the intimidating Darran Mountains, including Mt Tutoko (2723 m), and the upper Hollyford Valley. After a long sidle across these faces, the track zigzags sharply down to Lake Mackenzie, another of the track's highlights. The exquisitely coloured lake is surrounded by stunted and lichen-encrusted beech forest, with some large boulders – presumably glacier-deposited – around its edges. The imposing Emily Peak (1815 m) dominates the lake head. Lake Mackenzie Hut lies nearby.

Lake Mackenzie and Emily Peak

Lake Mackenzie Hut to The Divide via Lake Howden Hut 4–5.5 hours, 12 km

The last day of the Routeburn sidles through a pleasant diversity of scenery, past one sizeable waterfall (the 174 m-high Earland Falls), and through beech forest that becomes increasingly lush as you descend. En route, viewpoints offer striking vistas of the Hollyford Valley. At Lake Howden, a track diverts off into the Greenstone Valley (where there is a camping area at Greenstone Saddle). Past Lake Howden Hut (28 bunks, woodburner), the Routeburn Track begins to climb gradually up to a signposted turnoff to Key Summit (918 m). This 90-minute side-trip is the most outstanding on the track; the open knoll of Key Summit is studded with tarns and affords a complete 360-degree panorama of northern Fiordland.

Back on the Routeburn, the last hour of the track passes through increasingly moss-laden forest, gradually descending towards The Divide, where there is a shelter and toilets.

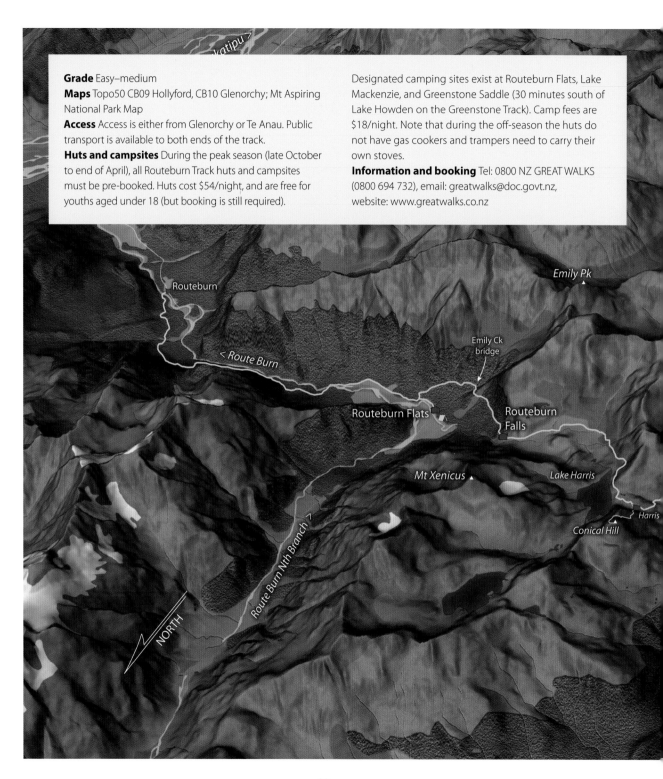

Grade Easy–medium

Maps Topo50 CB09 Hollyford, CB10 Glenorchy; Mt Aspiring National Park Map

Access Access is either from Glenorchy or Te Anau. Public transport is available to both ends of the track.

Huts and campsites During the peak season (late October to end of April), all Routeburn Track huts and campsites must be pre-booked. Huts cost $54/night, and are free for youths aged under 18 (but booking is still required).

Designated camping sites exist at Routeburn Flats, Lake Mackenzie, and Greenstone Saddle (30 minutes south of Lake Howden on the Greenstone Track). Camp fees are $18/night. Note that during the off-season the huts do not have gas cookers and trampers need to carry their own stoves.

Information and booking Tel: 0800 NZ GREAT WALKS (0800 694 732), email: greatwalks@doc.govt.nz, website: www.greatwalks.co.nz

katipu

Emily Pk

Routeburn

< Route Burn

Emily Ck
bridge

Routeburn Flats

Routeburn
Falls

Mt Xenicus

Lake Harris

Harris

Conical Hill

Route Burn Nth Branch

NORTH

Greenstone
Track

AILSA MOUNTAINS

Earland
Falls

Lake Howden

Lake Howden

Key
Summit

The Divide

94

Lake
Mackenzie

Mackenzie

an Pk

< Hollyford R. / Whakatipu Kā Tuka

rahaka Whakatipu

DARRAN MOUNTAINS

HOLLYFORD TRACK
FIORDLAND NATIONAL PARK 5–9 DAYS

The Hollyford Track offers two things that most tracks in precipitous Fiordland rarely do: easy, flat travel that nowhere exceeds 150 m above sea-level, and a delightful coastal section (at Martins Bay) where you can actually rub your feet in both sand and sea.

Aside from the delights of Martins Bay, where you might see penguins or fur seals, and those sections that skirt Lake McKerrow/Whakatipu Waitai, most of the track passes through lush, dense forest, often dominated by podocarps.

Trampers who are veterans of the Kepler, Milford or Routeburn tracks might imagine the Hollyford's lowland terrain will offer few vistas, but in fact significant sections of it have spectacular views of the Darran Mountains, Fiordland's highest and most glaciated range. Best of all, the Hollyford can be walked comfortably in any season, allowing trampers a chance to avoid the sandfly-infested months of summer.

As the Hollyford Track is a not a circuit, walking it involves a tramp in both directions (62 km each way). However, those willing to indulge in some mechanical assistance can reach Martins Bay by plane, thus avoiding the outward journey. Jet-boats also operate between Martins Bay and McKerrow Island Huts. Guided walks are possible, using private huts, but only the independent option is described here.

Hollyford Road Shelter to Hidden Falls Hut (12 bunks, woodburner) 2–3 hours, 9 km

From the shelter, follow an old road, soon crossing Humboldt Creek on a bridge. From here, the well-benched track heads northwards, sidling bluffs beside an extensive wetland on the floor of the Hollyford Valley. A raised boardwalk avoids the flood-prone section. After about 90 minutes, the track again reaches the banks of the Hollyford River/Whakatipu Ka Tuka, which is followed reasonably closely as far as Hidden Falls Creek. Fifteen minutes before Hidden Falls Hut, you cross a footbridge near Hidden Falls, impressive more for their volume than for their height. The clearing at Hidden Falls Hut offers good views of the Darran Mountains, noticeably Mt Madeline (2536 m), Fiordland's second-highest peak.

Hidden Falls Hut to Lake Alabaster Hut (26 bunks, woodburner) 3–4 hours, 10.5 km

From Hidden Falls Hut, the track passes through flat, forested terrain and climbs very gradually over Little Homer Saddle, at 143 m the highest point on the track. Views of Mt Tutoko, Fiordland's highest peak (2723 m), open up at a lookout en route. On the far side of the saddle, the track descends gently to pass Little Homer Falls (60 m). More flat travel leads to a short section beside the Hollyford River/Whakatipu Ka Tuka, then beyond to where the trail branches up the Pyke River, a major tributary. If you wish to stay at Lake Alabaster Hut, do not cross a substantial footbridge over the Pyke, but keep going for a further 20 minutes. Alabaster Hut lies near the shore of Lake Alabaster/Wawahi Waka.

Opposite Lake McKerrow/Whakatipu Waitai at dawn

Lake Alabaster Hut to Demon Trail Hut (12 bunks, woodburner) 5–6 hours, 14.7 km

The next two sections of track, as far as Hokuri Hut, are rougher and muddier than the previous sections. From Lake Alabaster Hut, return to the footbridge over the Pyke River, where the main Hollyford Track continues. Easy – although sometimes muddy – travel leads through forest down the Hollyford Valley towards Lake McKerrow/Whakatipu Waitai. McKerrow Island Hut (12 bunks, woodburner) is accessible on a side-track, but reaching it requires crossing a flood channel of the Hollyford River/Whakatipu Ka Tuka, which may be impassable after rain.

Lake McKerrow/Whakatipu Waitai was once a fiord similar to those further south, but at Martins Bay the fiord mouth gradually in-filled, leaving the freshwater lake behind it. The so-called 'Demon Trail' skirts the shores of the lake, and while it is rocky, occasionally muddy and more undulating than the rest of the Hollyford Track, it's hardly hellish. Demon Trail Hut lies in a small clearing about 90 minutes beyond the McKerrow Island Hut turnoff. On a good day the nearby lakeshore offers fine views of the Darran Mountains.

Demon Trail Hut to Hokuri Hut (20 bunks, woodburner) 5–6 hours, 9.6 km

From Demon Trail Hut, continue along the Demon Trail, which offers occasional views over Lake McKerrow/Whakatipu Waitai. Several streams draining the nearby Skippers Range are crossed: the first on a footbridge and three on walk-wires. Near Hokuri Hut, the trail begins to flatten out again.

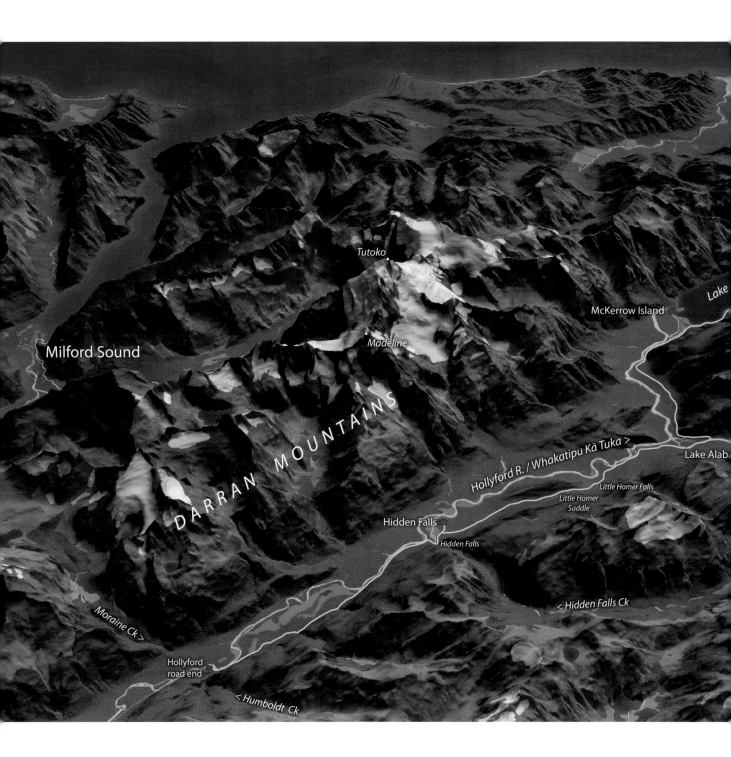

Milford Sound

Tutoko

Madeline

McKerrow Island

Lake

DARRAN MOUNTAINS

Hollyford R. / Whakatipu Kā Tuka >

Lake Alab

Little Homer Falls

Little Homer
Saddle

Hidden Falls

Hidden Falls

< Hidden Falls Ck

Moraine Ck >

Hollyford
road end

< Humboldt Ck

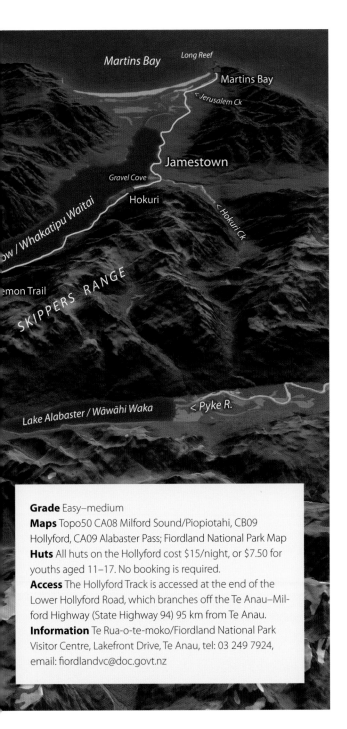

Martins Bay Long Reef

Martins Bay

< Jerusalem Ck

Jamestown

Gravel Cove

Hokuri

< Hokuri Ck

ow / Whakatipu Waitai

SKIPPERS RANGE

emon Trail

Lake Alabaster / Wāwāhi Waka   < Pyke R.

Hokuri Hut to Martins Bay Hut (24 bunks, wood-burner) 4–5 hours, 13 km

From Hokuri Hut, the Hollyford Track passes Gravel Cove, then heads up the sizeable Hokuri Creek to a walk-wire. Once across, the track skirts the last section of Lake McKerrow/Whakatipu Waitai, passing through Jamestown, the site of a failed settlement established in 1870, where now there are just a few private baches. From the point where the track leaves the lake for the final time, it cuts across forested flats, past an airstrip. Beyond, scrubby travel leads to Jerusalem Creek, which can be difficult to cross when in flood. Soon, the whiff of sea air becomes noticeable for the first time. The last section of the track skirts a tidal section of the Hollyford River/Whakatipu Ka Tuka, reaching the sea at Martins Bay Hut. This is a place to spend at least two days, exploring the rocky coastline, and enjoying the outlook over the extensive sandbar that forms Martins Bay. Between July and November, trampers might encounter Fiordland crested penguins and New Zealand fur seals at Long Reef.

Fur seals, Martins Bay

Grade Easy–medium
Maps Topo50 CA08 Milford Sound/Piopiotahi, CB09 Hollyford, CA09 Alabaster Pass; Fiordland National Park Map
Huts All huts on the Hollyford cost $15/night, or $7.50 for youths aged 11–17. No booking is required.
Access The Hollyford Track is accessed at the end of the Lower Hollyford Road, which branches off the Te Anau–Milford Highway (State Highway 94) 95 km from Te Anau.
Information Te Rua-o-te-moko/Fiordland National Park Visitor Centre, Lakefront Drive, Te Anau, tel: 03 249 7924, email: fiordlandvc@doc.govt.nz

KEPLER TRACK
FIORDLAND NATIONAL PARK 3–4 DAYS

Although tracks had existed in the eastern Kepler Mountains since the nineteenth century, it was not until the mid-1980s that the idea for a tourist track – the Kepler Track – was developed. The initial plan was to create a high-quality walk to reduce pressure on the increasingly popular Milford and Routeburn tracks. Soon after it was opened in February 1988, however, the Kepler Track rapidly became popular in its own right, and is now one of DOC's eight Great Walks. The 60 km track is easily accessible from the township of Te Anau. Essentially, it forms a circuit between the southernmost arm of Lake Te Anau and the northern reaches of Lake Manapouri.

On a good day, the tops section between Luxmore Hut and the Iris Burn Valley offers trampers superb views over Lake Te Anau's South Fiord, with the Murchison Mountains beyond. Lake Manapouri's beautiful island-studded waters form another highlight. The Kepler can be walked in either direction, but the anticlockwise route is described here.

Control gates to Luxmore Hut (50 bunks, wood-burner) 5–6 hours, 14 km

The Kepler Track begins and ends at the control gates, the outlet of Lake Te Anau.

For the first 90 minutes the track skirts close to the lakeshore, passing the pleasant Dock Bay before arriving at the Brod Bay Shelter and campsite. Beyond Brod Bay, the gentle start to the track is rudely brought to an end by a steepish 800 m climb up a face of Mt Luxmore.

Halfway up to the bushline is a viewpoint of Lake Te Anau. Higher up still, the track weaves beneath limestone bluffs, before finally emerging onto the tops. At an outstanding viewpoint, Lake Manapouri and the South Fiord first become visible. The large Luxmore Hut lies about 45 minutes beyond, reached by following a poled route. Once at the hut, those still with energy might want to visit the nearby Luxmore Cave (take a torch).

Luxmore Hut to Iris Burn Hut (54 bunks, wood-burner, gas cookers) 5–6 hours, 14.5 km

From Luxmore Hut, trampers face long sections of tops that are very exposed to bad weather. Although well marked by poles, this section should not be undertaken lightly when under snow or in poor visibility. If in doubt, spend another night at Luxmore Hut.

Initially, the track sidles through tussock grasslands, climbing gradually around Mt Luxmore. Keen trampers might like to take the 10-minute side-trip to the 1472-m summit.

Beyond, the track follows the ridge crest to Forest Burn Saddle, where there is a shelter and toilets. About another two hours' travel along the ridge leads to a second shelter at Hanging Valley. From Hanging Valley, the track begins a descent to the bushline down a series of steps, offering views of the upper Iris Burn and the rugged Kepler Mountains beyond. A steep, zigzagging descent leads down into the valley. Iris Burn Hut is situated in a pleasant beech-fringed clearing. The sizeable Iris Burn Falls can be reached after a 20-minute walk on a side-track.

Iris Burn Hut to Moturau Hut (40 bunks, wood-burner) 5–6 hours, 16 km

The third day of the Kepler basically follows the true left of the Iris Burn down to the shores of Lake Manapouri, and then around its shores to Moturau Hut. About 30 minutes after leaving Iris Burn Hut, the track crosses an open area opposite where a stupendous slip occurred in 1984, a sobering reminder of the Earth's forces.

Beyond, the track re-enters the forest. Several side streams are crossed on footbridges before you reach Rocky Point, where there is a toilet and a track workers' camp. Beyond Rocky Point, the track sidles through a small gorge in the Iris Burn, emerging on flats near the mouth of the river. Shortly after, the track first reaches the shores of Lake Manapouri, with Moturau Hut a further 30 minutes away.

Moturau Hut to Rainbow Reach 1.5–2 hours, 6 km

For those who don't wish to complete the entire circuit, the Kepler can be exited at Rainbow Reach. From Moturau Hut the track heads inland before reaching the Shallow Bay track junction. Highly recommended for those with spare time is the short 30-minute excursion to tranquil Shallow Bay, where there is a campsite and small hut (6 bunks).

Back at the track junction, the main Kepler Track continues, crossing a wetland (where there is a viewing platform) before reaching the Balloon Loop, then the sizeable Waiau River. The swingbridge leading to Rainbow Reach is a further 20 minutes on.

Above *Luxmore Hut in winter*

Rainbow Reach to control gates
2.5–3.5 hours, 9.5 km

For those diehards determined to complete the track, the Kepler heads northwards for another few hours, largely following the true right bank of the Waiau River. It's a flat, pleasant stroll through some fine forest, with regular views of the river.

Grade Medium

Maps Topo50 CD07 Manapouri, CD08 Te Anau; Fiordland National Park Map; Kepler Track Map

Access It's possible to walk along the shore of Lake Te Anau (5 km) to the control gates and the track start. Otherwise, organise a shuttle (these service both the control gates and Rainbow Reach). Water taxis can also be chartered to Brod Bay.

Huts and campsites During the peak season (late October to end of April), all Kepler Track huts and campsites must be pre-booked. Huts cost $54/night, and are free for youths aged under 18 (but booking is still required). Designated camping sites exist at Brod Bay and near Iris Burn Hut; camp fees are $18/night.

Information and booking Tel: 0800 NZ GREAT WALKS (0800 694 732), email: greatwalks@doc.govt.nz, website: www.greatwalks.co.nz

Lake Manapouri from the Kepler Track

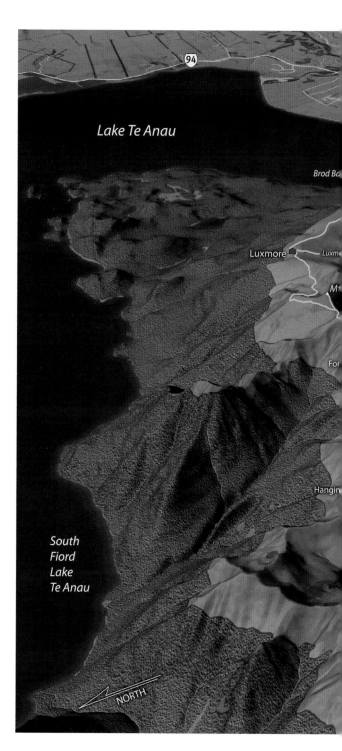

MILFORD TRACK
FIORDLAND NATIONAL PARK 4 DAYS

For almost a century the Milford has enjoyed a reputation as New Zealand's most famous track, a standing enhanced by its oft-repeated subtitle, 'The finest walk in the world'. Although this claim was made by an overly enthusiastic editor who'd never walked the track himself, the Milford's extraordinary scenery certainly ranks it on a global scale.

Despite being well formed and well graded, and in many places almost a seamless path, the 54 km Milford Track passes through some of the most precipitous country in Fiordland National Park. Beginning on a northern arm of Lake Te Anau, the track follows the Clinton River to its head, then over Mackinnon Pass to the Arthur Valley, ending on the shores of Milford Sound. In sunshine, the track is a delight of alpine scenery and mossy forests; in rain, the rivers become boisterous torrents and literally countless waterfalls tumble from the valley sides. One of these, the Sutherland Falls, cascades 580 m in three leaps, and ranks among the tallest in the world (recently, however, another Fiordland waterfall has eclipsed the Sutherland Falls' claim to be New Zealand's highest).

During the peak season, independent trampers must book the track well in advance, can only walk in the direction described, and must move on every day (a guided option using private huts is also possible).

Glade Wharf to Clinton Hut (40 bunks, wood-burner) 1–1.5 hours, 5 km

After the boat trip from Te Anau Downs, you disembark onto Glade Wharf on a northern arm of Lake Te Anau. Initially, the track has the width of a road, reaching the guided walk hut at Glade House after 30 minutes. Soon afterwards, you cross the Clinton River on a large footbridge, and the track narrows somewhat. Shortly before Clinton Hut, a side-track around the 'Wetland Walk' offers views over a colourful swamp of sphagnum moss.

Clinton Hut to Mintaro Hut (40 bunks, wood-burner) 6 hours, 16.5 km

From Clinton Hut, the track follows the true right bank of the Clinton River, passing through exquisitely mossy red beech forests, and reaches Clinton Forks after an hour. Beyond Clinton Forks, the track frequently breaks out into open shrubby areas with views of the steep glacier-carved valley sides. Numerous avalanche paths are obvious, and plenty of waterfalls tumble from high overhead. Hirere Shelter offers respite from the weather if it is raining, and a view of Hirere Falls. Beyond the guided walk hut at Pompolona, the track climbs briefly, crosses a footbridge, then begins a steady ascent through mossy forest to reach Lake Mintaro and Mintaro Hut. From the hut, Mackinnon Pass and the spectacular canyon-like walls of Mt Balloon dominate the views.

Mintaro Hut to Dumpling Hut (40 bunks, wood-burner) via Mackinnon Pass 6–7 hours, 14 km

Although not the longest day in distance, the climb of Mackinnon Pass and the side-trip to Sutherland Falls often make this day's tramp the longest. From Mintaro Hut, a 15-minute walk up the valley leads across flat terrain, until a footbridge over the now infant Clinton River is crossed. From here, the 400 m climb to the pass begins, up a series of switchbacks cut through the thinning forest. About two-thirds of the ascent is over once you reach the end of the shrub and forest line.

A stone monument to explorer Quintin Mackinnon sits in a commanding position on the pass crest. On a good day, Mts Balloon, Hart and Elliot all draw the eye, and from a nearby viewing area there is a giddy look down into the Arthur Valley. Another 100 m ascent is required to reach the highest point on the pass, and then it's a short descent to Mackinnon Pass Shelter.

The 1000 m descent into the Roaring Burn is not to be underestimated and takes considerable time. More switchbacks lead down to a footbridge over the Moraine Creek. From here, the track follows the true right of the Roaring Burn down to its junction with the Arthur River. Near the junction is the side-track leading to Quintin Lodge (a guided walk hut) and shelter. Leave your pack in the shelter for the very worthwhile 90-minute return trip to the base of the Sutherland Falls (580 m high). From Quintin Lodge, a further hour's tramping leads to Dumpling Hut.

Dumpling Hut to Sandfly Point 5–7 hours, 18 km

Downstream of Dumpling Hut, the track continues on the true right of the Arthur River as far as Boatshed Hut (a guided walk shelter), where it crosses a footbridge over the river. Mackay Falls, one of the most attractive waterfalls on the entire walk, is soon reached. Downstream of the falls, the track remains on the true left of the Arthur, sidling around the lengthy Lake Ada and passing the Giant Gate Falls (where there is a shelter) en route. Sections of this track are flood-prone.

Those waiting for a boat at the aptly named Sandfly Point will probably need to seek refuge in the nearby shelter. A collection of defunct boots adorns a signpost marking the end of the track.

Above *Forest and stream, Clinton Valley*

Milford
Sound

94

Sandfly Point

Lake Ada

Giant Gate Falls

Mackay
Falls

Boatshed (historic)

Mt Elliot

Mt Bo

Mack
P

Moraine Ck

Dumpling

Roaring Burn

< Arthur R.

Quintin Lodge

Sutherland
Falls

Glade House

Glade Wharf

Clinton

wetland walk

Clinton Forks

Clinton R.

Hirere Falls

Hirere

Prairie shelter

Bus Stop

Pompolona Lodge

Mintaro

Hart

ill

NORTH

Grade Medium

Maps Topo50 CB08 Homer Saddle; Fiordland National Park Map; Milford Track Map

Access Access is from Te Anau Downs, 27 km north of Te Anau on State Highway 94. Transport must be organised well in advance, at the same time as you book the track. From Te Anau, bus transport is available to Te Anau Downs, where a boat transports you to the track start at North Arm of Lake Te Anau. At the end of the track, boat transport is also required across Milford Sound to Milford Sound Village, which is regularly serviced by buses.

Huts During the peak season (late October to end of April), the Milford Track must be pre-booked, and this guarantees your place. Huts cost $54/night, and are free for youths aged under 18 (but booking is still required). No camping is allowed.

Information and booking Tel: 0800 NZ GREAT WALKS (0800 694 732), email: greatwalks@doc.govt.nz, website: www.greatwalks.co.nz

NORTH WEST CIRCUIT TRACK
RAKIURA NATIONAL PARK 8–12 DAYS

When it was created in 2002, Rakiura National Park became New Zealand's fourteenth national park. The 140,000 ha park encompasses 85 per cent of Stewart Island/Rakiura, the smallest of New Zealand's three main islands. Rakiura's North West Circuit Track offers trampers a rare opportunity to walk for several days along a natural coastline. While not a suitable tramp for novices, the circuit has a multitude of attractions: rugged granite coastlines, rimu and southern rata forests rising from a profusion of crown ferns, extensive wild dunelands and often radiant sunsets.

Although the tramping is not overly difficult, some of the long days require considerable stamina, and trampers need to be prepared to spend extended periods in mud. If you've tired of groomed trails, the North West Circuit will confirm that even DOC's expertise in track-making can't wholly tame the muddy wilds of Stewart Island/Rakiura. Trampers also have to carry food for eight days or more, and the resulting heavy packs will be a burden, especially in the mud, which can be waist-deep in the worst sections.

Aside from the superb coastal scenery, the island is well known for its birdlife. Trampers often see southern tokoeka – the kiwi present at Rakiura – wandering around during daylight hours, despite the birds' generally nocturnal habits. Kaka and kakariki are also present in greater numbers than on the mainland.

The North West Circuit Track can be walked in either direction, but the anticlockwise route gives a gentler introduction to the tramping. By the time you reach the longer, harder days on the western side of the island, your pack will be lighter and your fitness better. By catching a water taxi back from Freshwater Landing, trampers can shave off two days of walking at the end.

Lee Bay to Port William Hut (24 bunks, wood-burner) 4 hours, 12 km

From Halfmoon Bay (Oban), 90 minutes' walking on roads leads to Lee Bay. The first day of the North West Circuit Track follows a section of the Rakiura Track, one of DOC's eight Great Walks, where the standard of the path is high, with little mud. From Lee Bay, the track crosses forested terrain, mostly near the shore, until it emerges at the eastern end of Maori Beach. At the western end of Maori Beach, the track crosses a swingbridge over a tidal inlet, and climbs a headland around Wooding Bay, passing a turnoff to North Arm Hut en route. From here, the track descends to Magnetic Beach. Port William Hut is located at the northern end. The tall gum trees here are the sole remains of a failed attempt to settle the area in the 1870s.

Port William Hut to Bungaree Hut (16 bunks, woodburner) 3–4 hours, 6 km

From Port William Hut, the North West Circuit heads northwards. Near Sawyers Beach, the track crosses a footbridge and almost immediately heads inland again, cutting across forested terrain to Little Bungaree Beach. After crossing a footbridge, the track sidles beside a stream briefly before climbing over a low spur to Big Bungaree Beach. The hut lies near the northern end of the beach.

Tramper at West Ruggedy Beach

Bungaree Hut to Christmas Village Hut (12 bunks, woodburner) 5–6 hours, 11.5 km

From Bungaree Hut, the track crosses another forested ridge, then sidles to reach the southern end of Murray Beach. At the end of Murray Beach, the track heads inland, passing an excellent campsite and soon crossing a bridge. Near the bridge is an old steam-driven log-hauler, slowly being consumed by the forest but still in recognisable condition. From here, the track follows an old logging tramline through regenerating forest for about 30 minutes. For the next 90 minutes, the track traverses undulating forested terrain past Christmas Village Beach. Christmas Village Hut is a further 30 minutes beyond, situated on a bouldery bay.

Christmas Village Hut to Yankee River Hut (16 bunks, woodburner) 6–7 hours, 12 km

About 20 minutes after departing Christmas Village Hut, trampers reach the Mt Anglem/Hananui turnoff (those wanting to climb Mt Anglem/Hananui, which at 980 m is Stewart Island/Rakiura's highest peak, will require a whole day as the muddy 5.5 km track takes three to four hours to walk in each direction). For the next three hours, the track continues westwards, passing through some stands of rimu, with generally dry travel. After reaching the coastline again, it follows the length of Lucky Beach before heading inland for another three hours, again crossing undulating forested slopes with some tall stands of rimu. At Yankee River, a five-minute side-track leads down to Yankee River Hut.

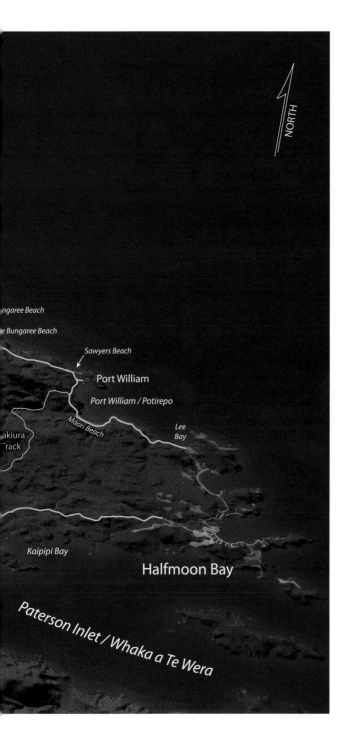

Yankee River Hut to Long Harry Hut (12 bunks, woodburner) 5 hours, 8.5 km

After crossing a swingbridge over the Yankee River, the track climbs 220 m over a forested knoll before descending to Smoky Beach. This is one of the longest beaches on the northern part of Stewart Island/Rakiura, with many sand dunes. At the western end of Smoky Beach is a flood route up to a swingbridge over Smoky Creek, but in most conditions trampers can simply cross the creek to the point where the track re-enters the forest. The track sidles across slopes cut by many small guts for about two hours before descending to Long Harry Hut, which lies at the eastern end of Long Harry Bay.

Long Harry Hut to East Ruggedy Hut (12 bunks, woodburner) 5–6 hours, 9.5 km

From Long Harry Hut, the track sidles above the coast, then descends to the old Long Harry Hut site (look out for kiwi on the track here). From here, it follows a forested ridge and then descends to a bouldery beach. At the beach's far end, the track climbs 200 m to a spectacular viewpoint overlooking East Ruggedy Beach, before descending steeply through manuka and muttonbird scrub to emerge at Ruggedy Stream. Don't be alarmed by the quicksand here – walk briskly until you are across the stream, then head up the valley for 20 minutes among dunes to reach East Ruggedy Hut.

East Ruggedy Hut to Big Hellfire Hut (12 bunks, woodburner) 7–8, hours, 14 km

In recent years, this section of the track has been considerably rerouted to make it easier, less muddy and more scenic. Shortly after leaving East Ruggedy Hut, the track crosses undulating forested terrain before descending through dunes to West Ruggedy Beach. This spectacular beach, with its granite pillars and rolling dunes, is followed for almost its entire length to the southern end. Offshore lie the aptly named Rugged Islands, looking like a rocky stack of toast about to collapse. The track follows the beach, but at high tide it may be necessary to scramble up over a rocky outcrop. Near the far end of the beach, the track enters forest to begin a slow sidle around the northern slopes of the Ruggedy Range. The route crosses the range through a low pass at about 240 m.

On the far side, a descent to bouldery Waituna Bay ensues. Good camping here offers vantage points of the low but impressive Ruggedy Mountains. Past Waituna Bay, the track climbs again, up onto a wide forested ridge, encountering probably the worst mud on the entire track. Improbably located at the top of an enormous sandhill some 200 m high, Big Hellfire Hut offers superb views of the Freshwater Flats.

Big Hellfire Hut to Mason Bay Hut (20 bunks, woodburner) 7–8 hours, 15 km

This is generally one of the more difficult and longest days on the circuit. Be sure to fill your water bottle at the hut. From Hellfire Pass, the track climbs gradually to a good viewpoint over the upper Freshwater Basin. Beyond, the track stays on the crest of a broad, dry ridge before beginning a gradual descent to Little Hellfire Beach. After crossing a stream, follow a short stretch of bouldery coastline until the track re-enters the forest. A 260 m climb leads over another headland, followed by a sharp descent to the northern end of the broad, sweeping Mason Bay.

Unless a high tide bars progress, head south along the beach for 90 minutes or so until the track leaves the coastline at Duck Creek, marked by a tall post. Mason Bay Hut lies 20 minutes inland, tucked into the back of the extensive dunes that characterise the bay.

Mason Bay Hut to Freshwater Hut (16 bunks, woodburner) 3–4 hours, 15.5 km

From Mason Bay Hut, the North West Circuit Track heads further inland, reaching the Island Hill Homestead after about 30 minutes. This was once the runholder's house when the Island Hill and Mason Bay area was a sheep run, but is now a DOC base. At night, it's a good place from which to listen for kiwi.

Flat, easy travel leads past Island Hill into manuka and tussock country sandwiched between forested hills. Basically, the track follows an old road and drain line used during the pastoral era, crossing an imperceptible saddle into the Freshwater catchment along the way. Thankfully, much of this section is boardwalked – a far cry from the days when the mud was of legendary status. Even so, after heavy rain parts of the track become waterlogged. Once across a footbridge near Scott Burn, the track cuts across more flat ground to finally reach the sizeable Freshwater River. Here, cross a swingbridge to reach Freshwater Hut. Although diehards may want to walk the last two days back to Halfmoon Bay (Oban), many trampers opt to arrange (in advance) a water taxi pick-up here.

Freshwater Hut to North Arm Hut (24 bunks, woodburner) 6–7 hours, 11 km

From Freshwater Hut, the track heads inland and then curls down the true left of the Freshwater River before making a significant 260 m climb over the Thomson Ridge and down the far side to the North Arm of Paterson Inlet/Whaka a Te Wera. Note that the track here can be slippery and arduous. Once reaching the coastline, the route stays near the shore, before joining the Rakiura Track at North Arm Hut.

North Arm Hut to Halfmoon Bay (Oban) 4 hours, 12 km

Now on the more groomed surface of the Rakiura Track, travel is quicker and easier. Undulating tramping through forest leads to historic Sawdust Bay, the scene of early sawmilling. From here, the track crosses a low headland to Kidney Fern Arm, then heads inland again until briefly skirting Kaipipi Bay. The last leg of the walk crosses a former road back to Halfmoon Bay (Oban).

Tramper overlooks the Gutter at the southern end of Mason Bay

Grade Hard
Maps Topo50 CH08 Codfish Island, CH09 Mount Anglem
Access Either fly or take the ferry to Halfmoon Bay (Oban), the only settlement on Stewart Island/Rakiura, where there is accommodation, a museum, cafés, a restaurant and a general store. Water taxis to Freshwater Landing operate from Halfmoon Bay (Oban).
Huts Aside from Port William and North Arm huts (which cost $22/night and require booking), all the huts on Stewart Island/Rakiura cost $5/night, or $2.50 for youths aged 11–17, and do not need to be booked.
Information Rakiura National Park Visitor Centre, 15 Main Road, Stewart Island/Rakiura, tel: 03 219 0009, email: stewartisland@doc.govt.nz. To book Port William and North Arm huts, tel: 0800 NZ GREAT WALKS (0800 694 732), email: greatwalks@doc.govt.nz, website: www.greatwalks.co.nz

Opposite *Christmas Village Hut* DARRYN PEGRAM/BLACK ROBIN PHOTOGRAPHY

CAPE BRETT TRACK
BAY OF ISLANDS, NORTHLAND 2–3 DAYS

The impressive headland of Cape Brett marks the eastern boundary of the scenic Bay of Islands, and is one of Northland's most popular coastal attractions. Some seven small peaks form the spine of the peninsula, said by Maori to represent the seven waka (canoes) in which the first Polynesians migrated to New Zealand.

In the days before automation, three families lived at the cape to service the prominent lighthouse. In 1996, DOC restored the one remaining keeper's cottage to serve as a hut, which now provides accommodation for one of Northland's best overnight tramping experiences. The hut, perched near the cape's tip, offers exceptional views of the three nearby islands: Otuwhanga, Motukokako (Piercy) and Tiheru (The Dog).

Trampers reach the hut on the Cape Brett Track, part of which is maintained by Cape Brett Walkways. While it is generally straightforward, the 16 km route takes a full day to complete, with a considerable amount of up and down travel, sometimes beside cliffs. Landing at Cape Brett itself is very subject to sea conditions, but disembarking at Deep Water Cove is usually possible.

Rawhiti to Deep Water Cove junction
5–6 hours, 10 km

From Rawhiti, the track climbs a series of stairs to the first viewpoint of the Cape Brett peninsula. Beyond, the track continues to climb steadily through regenerating forest typical of coastal Northland. After crossing one small stream, you reach the ridge crest at Pukehuia (345 m). Make sure you fill your water bottle from the water tank at the shelter here, as the track is dry for some distance after.

Beyond Pukehuia, the track passes a side-trail to Te Toroa Bay. Occasional viewpoints overlook the island-studded waters of the Bay of Islands. Beyond a grassy knoll at Pt 288 m, the track ambles down to a prominent track

> To avoid spreading kauri dieback disease, an easily spread pathogen that decimates kauri trees, please ensure you clean your boots thoroughly at the wash stations provided near track entrances.

junction. The left-hand branch leads to Deep Water Cove – a 30-minute side-trip to a very pleasant and sheltered cove with idyllic turquoise waters, where camping is possible.

Deep Water Cove junction to Cape Brett Hut
(23 bunks) 2–3 hours, 6 km

From the track junction, continue straight on into the Manawahuna Scenic Reserve. After crossing a stream, the track ascends to a lookout, where the cape comes into dramatic profile. Some impressive cliffs fall into the sea here, and it's rather daunting to see how far there is yet to go.

After sidling through forest, the track crosses close to Ohututea Bay before beginning a steady haul up to a grassy saddle flanked by cliffs on both sides of the peninsula. From here, the last kilometre or so traverses a razorback ridge up to a knoll, from where there are astounding views of the lighthouse, the cape and the offshore islands. The final stretch zigzags through grass to the hut, which is perched on a prominent flat overlooking the ocean. On rare calm days, it's possible to swim and sometimes observe dolphins.

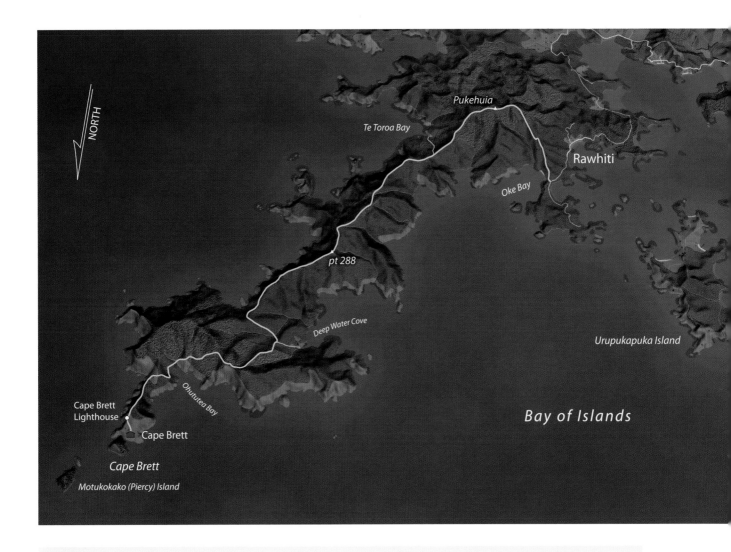

Grade Medium–hard

Maps Topo50 AV30 Cape Brett

Access The track begins at Oke Bay, Rawhiti, which is 26 km from Russell. The section of the track between Rawhiti and Deep Water Cove crosses land administered by Cape Brett Walkways, who charge a track maintenance fee of $30 per person ($15 for children), payable to DOC when you book the hut. Cape Brett Walkways also offer a guided walk option.

Hut Cape Brett Hut (gas cookers supplied) costs $15/night, or $7.50 for youths aged 11–17, and must be booked in advance. After booking, DOC will provide the keypad combination to unlock the door.

Information DOC Pewhairangi/Bay of Islands, 34 Landing Road, Kerikeri, tel: 09 407 0300, email: bayofislandsbooking@ doc.govt.nz. Cape Brett Walkways, tel: 09 403 8020, email: info@russellinfo.co.nz, website: www.capebrettwalks.co.nz

AOTEA TRACK
AOTEA CONSERVATION PARK, GREAT BARRIER ISLAND
(AOTEA ISLAND) 2 DAYS

In 2015, New Zealand's most recent conservation park, the Aotea Conservation Park, was officially opened on Great Barrier Island (Aotea Island), the largest landmass off the North Island's coast. While getting to Great Barrier (Aotea) presents some logistical challenges, even for Auckland trampers, the island offers this enjoyable overnight walk, which has a bit of everything: a snatch of coastline, distinctive volcanic topography and some fine regenerating kauri forest. Because Great Barrier (Aotea) has remained free of possums and stoats, the birdlife is prolific too, with flocks of screeching kaka and chattering kakarirki particularly noticeable.

Like the Coromandel Peninsula, Great Barrier (Aotea) experienced a long kauri logging era. The rugged terrain of the Kaiaraara Valley proved to be the least accessible, but using ingenious timber dams, loggers managed to strip all the remaining kauri in just three years between 1926 and 1929, excepting that on the summit of Mt Hobson, the island's highest point.

The Aotea Track offers trampers a circuit over Mt Hobson, with unsurpassed views of the Hauraki Gulf. It's described here as a circuit beginning near Port Fitzroy, where the ferry disembarks. However, if you are flying to Great Barrier (Aotea) it is probably better to arrange a taxi to Windy Canyon and Palmers Track, and tramp to Mt Heale Hut that way, then exit out to the airport at Claris via the Peach Tree Track.

Road end to Kaiaraara Hut (28 bunks, wood-burner) 20–30 minutes, 2 km

The track begins on an old logging road, appropriately enough called Forest Road, which follows the true right side of Kaiaraara Stream. It passes through forest, dominated at first by manuka, until reaching a large footbridge over the stream. Cross here to reach Kaiaraara Hut a short distance beyond.

Kaiaraara Hut to Mt Heale Hut (28 bunks, wood-burner) via Mt Hobson 3–4 hours, 6 km

Cross back over the footbridge, and resume walking on the well-graded and well-benched track, which passes through lush subtropical forest, with nikau palms and regenerating kauri notably conspicuous.

The track climbs gradually, crossing the stream a number of times on footbridges. Past a junction with the Coopers

Castle Track, it begins to steepen. Sadly, a flash flood in 2014 destroyed New Zealand's largest remaining kauri dam, which was located about halfway up the Kaiaraara Stream. Built in 1926, it had been restored by DOC, and was one of the highlights of the Aotea Track.

Higher up are spectacular views of volcanic rhyolitic outcrops, beyond which an extensive series of wooden stairs climbs the steeper slopes leading to the summit of Mt Hobson. Shortly before the summit, the track reaches a signposted junction where the Palmers Track/Windy Canyon route (the alternative way to start the tramp; see above) branches off.

A five-minute side-track leads to Mt Hobson (621 m), where, on a fine day, the summit viewing platform offers superlative views of Te Hauturu-o-Toi/Little Barrier Island and the numerous other islands of the Hauraki Gulf. The summit also boasts the island's largest remaining section of

Grade Medium

Map Topo50 AY34 Claris

Access Regular ferries operate from Auckland to Port Fitzroy. Alternatively, flights land at Claris. Shuttle operators offer services to take you to the track start.

Huts Both Kaiaraara and Mt Heale huts cost $15/night, or $7.50 for youths aged 11–17. Booking is required (www.doc.govt.nz).

Information and booking

Tamaki Makaurau/Auckland Visitor Centre, 137 Quay Street, Princes Wharf, Auckland, tel: 09 379 6476, email: aucklandvc@doc.govt.nz. For information on Great Barrier transport and accommodation, visit www.thebarrier.co.nz

virgin kauri forest, a number of rare plants, and a population of black petrels that nest here between October and June.

Beyond the summit, the main track descends more wooden stairs, steeply in places, with the spire of Mt Heale dominating the landscape. Mt Heale Hut is located on the mountain's southern side. A large, modern DOC hut with a veranda, it offers excellent views over the western forests and harbours of Great Barrier (Aotea) and also Te Hauturu-o-Toi/Little Barrier islands.

Mt Heale Hut to Kaiaraara Hut via South Fork Track 2–3 hours, 5 km

This section requires fording the Kaiaraara Stream twice, which can be impassable after heavy rain. If in doubt, it's probably best to exit via the all-weather Peach Tree Track. From Mt Heale Hut, the track follows a ridge through regenerating forest to a signposted junction, where the Peach Tree Track branches off (an alternative exit to Claris that passes the Kaitoke Hot Springs en route). Take the South Fork Track, which descends to cross a swingbridge over a tributary, with views back to Mt Heale and the hut. Beyond, the track descends steadily, sidling across steep bush faces, with handrails in one or two places. Eventually, it reaches the south fork in the Kaiaraara Stream. After fording, the track continues downstream, past the site of another former kauri dam. A second ford across the Kaiaraara Stream leads to a short but sharp ascent to the benched Forest Road. Kaiaraara Hut is another 20 minutes further along.

To avoid spreading kauri dieback disease, an easily spread pathogen that decimates kauri trees, please ensure you clean your boots thoroughly at the wash stations provided near track entrances.

PINNACLES HUT AND THE KAUAERANGA KAURI TRAIL

COROMANDEL FOREST PARK 2 DAYS

In the mid-2000s, scientists studying satellite imagery upset Northland's long-held claim as the kauri capital of New Zealand when it found that the Coromandel Peninsula in fact has a greater area under kauri forest. In some ways it is a miracle that any of these magnificent trees survived at all. As late as the 1920s, loggers were felling some of the least-accessible kauri trees on the peninsula, using ingenious but destructive kauri dam technology. Kauri dams were the result of Canadian lumberjack techniques adapted to New Zealand conditions. The clever design allowed kauri logs to be flushed out of the steep, volcanic country using a tripping mechanism that released the front wall of the dam. About a hundred of these dams were built in the Coromandel Range's Kauaeranga Valley, some 18 km inland from Thames, where residents could sometimes hear the boom of logs tumbling down in a flood of water.

New Zealand's best-preserved kauri dam forms the central attraction of this increasingly popular track, known as the Kauaeranga Kauri Trail. A walk to Pinnacles Hut, New Zealand's largest backcountry hut, offers a snapshot experience of the Coromandel Range, with its regenerating kauri forests, volcanic topography and fascinating history.

Dancing Camp kauri dam

Road end to Hydro Camp via Webb Creek
2–2.5 hours, 3.5 km

From the road end, the well-graded track crosses the Kauaeranga River on a swingbridge, then climbs steadily beside Webb Creek, passing some attractive falls and a few footbridges en route. After about two hours, the track reaches the Hydro Camp, a base used by workers erecting power lines over the range in the 1940s. From here, take the signposted route towards Pinnacles Hut.

Hydro Camp to Pinnacles Hut (80 bunks)
60 minutes, 2.5 km

From the Hydro Camp, the track sidles and climbs through more regenerating kauri forest, eventually cresting the broad tops of the Coromandel Range, with a view of Pinnacles Hut and The Pinnacles. A short descent leads to the hut. Nearby, a short walk leads to Dancing Camp dam (built in 1924), the second largest of all the kauri dams that were constructed in the valley. DOC staff partially restored the dam in 1994.

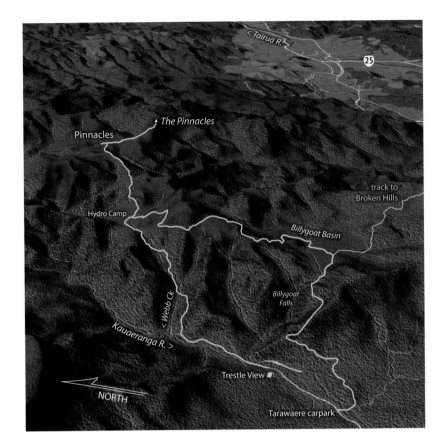

Grade Easy–medium

Map Topo50 BB35 Hikua

Access The track begins 23 km from Thames. Turn off State Highway 25 onto the Kauaeranga Valley Road, 2 km south of Thames, then follow the winding road for 13 km to the excellent DOC visitor centre, which gives good information on the valley's history and conservation values. The road ends a further 8 km up the valley, past several campgrounds and picnic areas.

Hut and camping Pinnacles Hut costs $15/night or $7.50 for youths aged 11–17, and must be booked well in advance of your trip. The Kauaeranga Valley has several camping areas; all have toilets, drinking water and picnic tables.

Information DOC Kauaeranga Visitor Centre, Kauaeranga Valley Road, Thames, tel: 07 867 9080, email: kauaerangavc@doc.govt.nz

Return climb to The Pinnacles
30–60 minutes, 1 km each way

A popular side-trip from the hut is the 1 km climb up to The Pinnacles (773 m). This section is steeper than the rest of the trail, with ladders and grab rungs in some places. However, once on top your effort is rewarded by a superb panorama over the surrounding range, with the ocean visible on either side of the Coromandel Peninsula.

Hydro Camp to road end via Billygoat Track
3–3.5 hours, 7 km

From Pinnacles Hut, return to the Hydro Camp. Here, the Kauri Trail continues to Billygoat Basin, along the way passing a clearing with a basic campsite, and the site of two historic trestle bridges. Shortly beyond, take the right-hand branch of a track junction to reach a viewpoint overlooking the 180 m-high Billygoat Falls. During the 1880s, many kauri logs were wastefully smashed over these falls. Later, during the 1920s, a tramway was built down the 'Billygoat Incline', enabling a steam hauler to lower kauri logs safely down to the valley. DOC has restored one section of the incline.

Lower down, the track reaches gentler gradients, and finally fords the Kauaeranga River to the Tarawaere carpark. The main track start is just 300 m back up the road, at the Trestle View Campground.

To avoid spreading kauri dieback disease, an easily spread pathogen that decimates kauri trees, please ensure you clean your boots thoroughly at the wash stations provided near track entrances.

LAKE WAIKAREMOANA TRACK
TE UREWERA 3–5 DAYS

One of New Zealand's eight Great Walks, the Lake Waikaremoana Track partially circumnavigates one of the country's most enchanting lakes. Set in the North Island's largest remaining tract of forest, the 46 km track passes through mixed beech–podocarp forest, home to a good diversity of native birds, skirting the lake shore in places and crossing over numerous small peninsulas in others. Panekire Bluff, the highest point on the track, offers superlative views over the lake and the northern forests of Te Urewera beyond.

Although the track is a Great Walk, its surface is less tailored than some of its southern counterparts and often has a backcountry flavour. During summer, the route is popular, while the quieter winter months see fewer walkers. The description below follows the clockwise direction, beginning from Onepoto on the lake's southeastern corner, although walking it anticlockwise is just as preferable.

Onepoto to Panekire Hut (36 bunks)
4–6 hours, 9 km

The track starts a short distance up a side road at Onepoto, accessible from State Highway 38, where the Onepoto Shelter provides a place to sort gear. Initially, the track climbs steadily through forest, gaining height with relative ease, until the first viewpoint opens out. The lake's various arms stretch in several directions, hinting at their origins as drowned river valleys (the lake was created by a landslide some 2200 years ago).

Most of the climbing is accomplished by Pt 964 m, and beyond here the track follows the ridge crest, with regular viewpoints. Shortly before Panekire Hut, a series of wooden steps negotiates a steep section of cliff. Panekire Hut is the highest hut on the track, and sits perched on a terrace not far from the bluff edge.

Panekire Hut to Waiopaoa Hut (30 bunks)
3–4 hours, 8 km

Beyond Panekire Hut, the track continues along the Panekire Range, weaving among some exquisitely twisted and mossy silver beech trees. After undulating for several kilometres, it drops off on a spur towards the lake and Waiopaoa Hut. The hut is set back from the lake edge adjacent to the Waiopaoa campsite.

Waiopaoa Hut to Marauiti Hut (26 bunks)
4.5–5 hours, 12 km

From Waiopaoa Hut the track skirts the shore at first. After about 60–90 minutes a side-trail branches off to the 22 m-high Korokoro Falls – a diversion well worth the effort (allow 60 minutes return). Back on the main track, cross a large footbridge over the Korokoro Stream to reach the Korokoro campsite. Beyond the camp, the track sidles around some steeper parts of the lake, crossing numerous streams. After the track rounds Te Kotoreotaunoa Point, it makes a long detour up a valley that drains into Maraunui Bay. You can see your destination on the opposite bank for some time before you reach it. At Maraunui there's a substantial truck workers' base, with the Maraunui campsite nearby. Marauiti Hut is located across a small peninsula, occupying a tranquil and secluded corner of Marauiti Bay, one of the lake's most scenic spots.

Marauiti Hut to Waiharuru Hut (40 bunks)
2 hours, 6.5 km

After leaving Marauiti Hut, the track climbs over another peninsula, passes Te Totara and Ahimanu bays, and then sidles across to an inlet at Upokororo Bay. Waiharuru, the largest of the track's huts, is located here with a camping area nearby. Panekire Bluff can be seen on the far side of the lake.

Lake Waikaremoana from the Panekire Range

Waiharuru Hut to Whanganui Hut (18 bunks)
2 hours, 6.5 km

Beyond Waiharuru Hut, the track soon crosses another large footbridge, then sidles around the shore before a significant ascent crosses a neck of the Puketukutuku Peninsula. A predator-control programme on this peninsula aims to protect North Island brown kiwi, which may be heard in the evening.

On the other side of the peninsula you reach the final camping area, Tapuaenui. From here, the track follows the lake once again, now in the Whanganui Inlet, through patches of kanuka interspersed with beech. Whanganui Hut, the smallest of those on the Great Walk, lies at the inlet head.

Whanganui Hut to Hopuruahine road end
1.5 hours, 4 km

From Whanganui Hut the track meanders around the shore for an hour or so, then crosses the Hopuruahine Stream via a footbridge to reach the road. A water-taxi landing is passed en route.

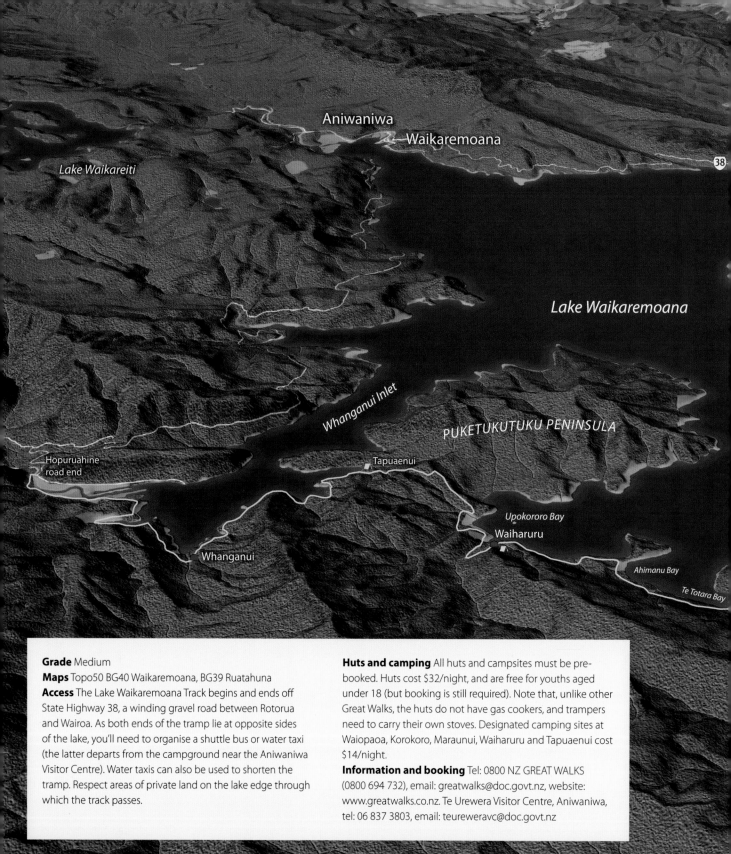

Aniwaniwa

Waikaremoana

Lake Waikareiti

38

Lake Waikaremoana

Whanganui Inlet

PUKETUKUTUKU PENINSULA

Hopuruahine
road end

Tapuaenui

Upokororo Bay

Waiharuru

Whanganui

Ahimanu Bay

Te Totara Bay

Grade Medium

Maps Topo50 BG40 Waikaremoana, BG39 Ruatahuna

Access The Lake Waikaremoana Track begins and ends off State Highway 38, a winding gravel road between Rotorua and Wairoa. As both ends of the tramp lie at opposite sides of the lake, you'll need to organise a shuttle bus or water taxi (the latter departs from the campground near the Aniwaniwa Visitor Centre). Water taxis can also be used to shorten the tramp. Respect areas of private land on the lake edge through which the track passes.

Huts and camping All huts and campsites must be pre-booked. Huts cost $32/night, and are free for youths aged under 18 (but booking is still required). Note that, unlike other Great Walks, the huts do not have gas cookers, and trampers need to carry their own stoves. Designated camping sites at Waiopaoa, Korokoro, Maraunui, Waiharuru and Tapuaenui cost $14/night.

Information and booking Tel: 0800 NZ GREAT WALKS (0800 694 732), email: greatwalks@doc.govt.nz, website: www.greatwalks.co.nz. Te Urewera Visitor Centre, Aniwaniwa, tel: 06 837 3803, email: teureweravc@doc.govt.nz

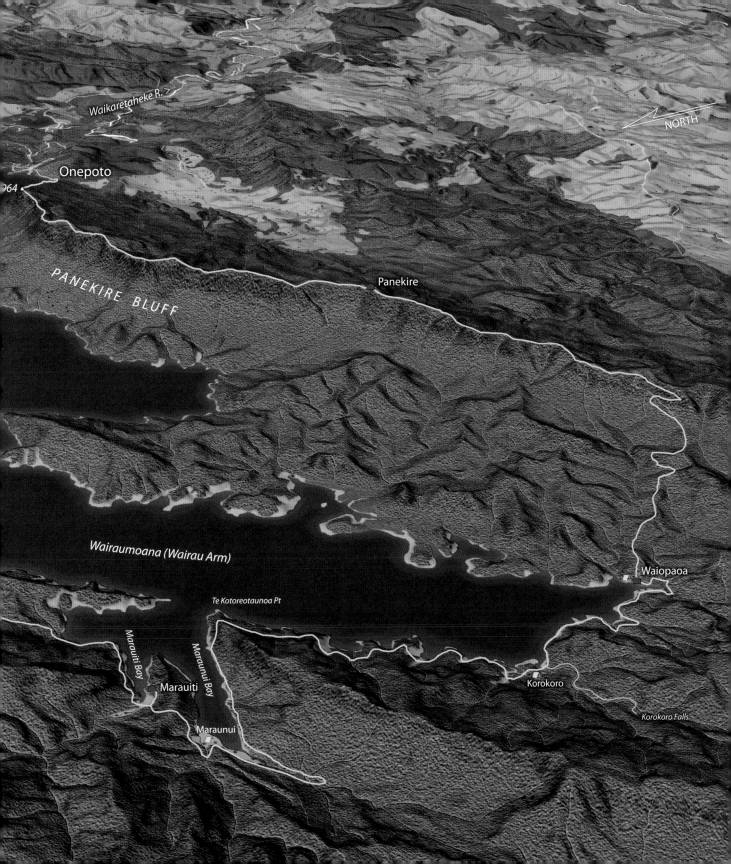

Waikaretaheke R.

NORTH

Onepoto

064

PANEKIRE BLUFF

Panekire

Wairaumoana (Wairau Arm)

Waiopaoa

Te Kotoreotaunoa Pt

Marauiti Bay

Maraunui Bay

Marauiti

Korokoro

Korokoro Falls

Maraunui

LAKE WAIKAREITI
TE UREWERA 2 DAYS

Accessible Lake Waikareiti, a small island-studded lake in Te Urewera, makes an ideal destination for families or those seeking an easy overnight walk. Like its larger neighbour, Waikaremoana, Lake Waikareiti was formed by a landslide. The lake's one hut, Sandy Bay, is located on the northeastern shore, and can be reached via the tramp described here, or by the alternative Ruapani Track. Unfortunately, the option of hiring a row boat is no longer possible.

Birdlife is good in Te Urewera forests, and on your tramp you may encounter kaka, kakariki, kereru, riflemen, tomtits and robins. During the night at Sandy Bay, there's also a chance to hear North Island brown kiwi.

Aniwaniwa to Lake Waikareiti Shelter
1 hour, 3.5 km

The well-benched and well-graded track to Lake Waikareiti begins just a couple of hundred metres from the Aniwaniwa Visitor Centre. Climbing slowly through dense forest, it crosses a number of small streams on footbridges before cresting a lip to arrive at the lake edge. A basic shelter provides a place to rest.

Lake Waikareiti Shelter to Sandy Bay Hut
(18 bunks) 3 hours, 7 km

The Lake Waikareiti Track sidles away from the lake, passing through a mixture of red and silver beech with the occasional rimu. Past the turnoff to the Ruapani Track, the route approaches the lake edge once again at Tawari Bay, offering views of the lake's islands. From the last viewpoint, the track begins an extensive sidle quite some distance from the lake, which is not reached again until Sandy Bay. Ten minutes before reaching the bay, you pass a track that branches off to Kaipo Lagoon (a pleasant two-hour return trip). Sandy Bay offers good, although cool, swimming. The three-roomed hut is large with a pleasant veranda from which to admire dawn or dusk over the lake.

Sandy Bay Hut to Aniwaniwa via Ruapani Track
6–7 hours, 14 km

The Ruapani Track offers trampers an alternative – although longer – way to tramp back to Aniwaniwa. It branches off the main track beyond Tawari Bay, passing several small lakes and wetlands en route, and eventually ends near the visitor centre. There are some exquisite forest scenes en route.

Overhanging beech trees, Sandy Bay, Lake Waikareiti

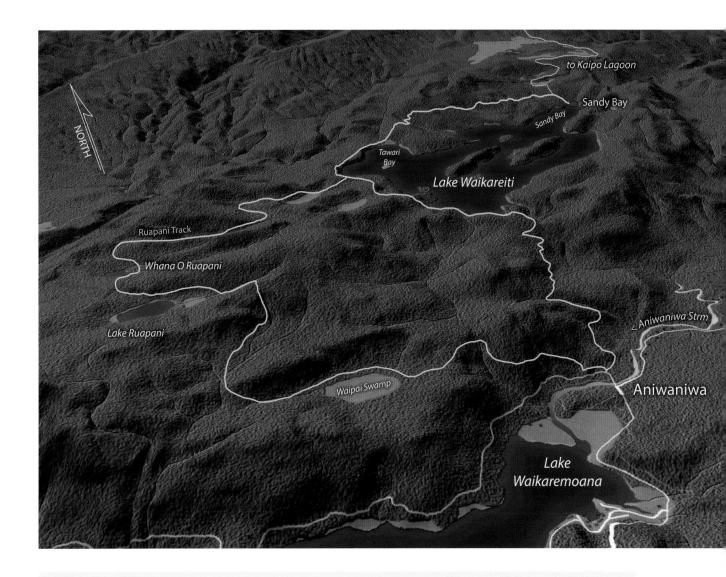

Grade Easy–medium

Map Topo50 BG40 Waikaremoana

Access From State Highway 2 at Wairoa, turn off onto State Highway 38, which leads to Lake Waikaremoana. At the small village of Waikaremoana there's a motor camp and shop, and shortly afterwards you reach the Aniwaniwa Visitor Centre, which has information and toilets.

Hut Sandy Bay Hut costs $15/night, or $7.50 for youths aged 11–17, and must be booked.

Information and booking Sandy Bay hut can be booked on the DOC website www.doc.govt.nz or through the Te Urewera Visitor Centre, Aniwaniwa, tel: 06 837 3803, email: teureweravc@doc.govt.nz

CENTRAL WHIRINAKI HUT
WHIRINAKI TE PUA-A-TANE FOREST PARK 3 DAYS

Whirinaki in the Bay of Plenty is renowned for the conservation battles that occurred there in the late 1970s and early 1980s. Determined conservationists fought to save some of the finest podocarp forests in the country, which the New Zealand Forest Service planned to cut for timber. Podocarps, including rimu, kahikatea, totara, miro and matai, occur in the Whirinaki Valley at a density rarely encountered elsewhere, forming a unique glimpse into the type of forests that once dominated Gondwana some 150 million years ago. After spirited debate, protests and tension with the local community at Minginui, conservationists – helped by a change in government – won the day. Whirinaki Te Pua-a-Tane Forest Park was created in 1984, and has since become a favourite haunt of trampers. The 36 km track described here forms a convenient loop and includes two huts, one each in the Mangamate and Whirinaki valleys.

River Road to Mangamate Hut (9 bunks, woodburner) 3.5–4 hours, 10 km

From the carpark, a well-benched and well-graded track leads through a magnificent section of forest dominated by all five of the major podocarp species. After about 15 minutes, the track crosses the Whirinaki River on a footbridge, providing a good view of the spectacular ignimbrite gorge known as Te Whaiti Nui A Toi Canyon.

Upstream, the track follows terraces on the true right of the river, soon passing the turnoff to Moerangi Hut. An hour's tramping leads to another track junction, signposted near a footbridge. Head left here towards Mangamate Hut. This section of track is noticeably rougher, following the course of the Mangamate River, with frequent river crossings. The last section sidles and climbs on the flanks of a forested ridge, reaching the head of Mangamate Stream, where Mangamate Hut is located in a small clearing on a forested saddle.

Mangamate Hut to Central Whirinaki Hut (24 bunks, woodburner) 3–4 hours, 9 km

The track drops immediately into the headwaters of the Kakanui Stream, and follows this for some distance before climbing over another forested saddle into the Taumutu Stream, another tributary of the Whirinaki River. More stream travel ensues, through a stand of stately red beech trees, before you reach a track junction. Keep heading downstream, following the sign to Central Whirinaki Hut (unless you're planning to visit Upper Whirinaki Hut, which lies upstream). At the confluence of the Taumutu and Whirinaki, pass a track and footbridge leading off to the left (to the Whirinaki Caves), and continue down the valley. The track becomes wide and well benched again. Central Whirinaki Hut is a large and popular hut with plenty of campsites nearby.

Central Whirinaki Hut to River Road 5–6 hours, 17 km

From Central Whirinaki Hut, the flat, gentle track leads down the true right of the Whirinaki River, passing through some exquisitely tall and elegant trees in places. En route, several footbridges cross side streams, and one short five-minute side-trip leads to a viewpoint of the 8 m-high Whirinaki Falls. Not far beyond the falls is the Mangamate Track junction. With the round trip now complete, it is just an amble back past the canyon and across the river to the carpark.

Minginui

Whirinaki R.

River Road

Te Whaiti Nui A Toi Canyon

Whirinaki Falls

Mangamate Strm. >

Whirinaki R. >

Moerangi

< Kakanui Strm

Mangamate

Central Whirinaki

< Whirinaki R.

< Taumutu Strm

NORTH

to Whirinaki Caves,
Plateau Rd

to
Upper Whirinaki Hut

Grade Easy–medium

Maps Topo50 BG38 Wairapukao, BG39 Ruatahuna

Access Whirinaki Te Pua-a-Tane Forest Park is 90 km from Rotorua and accessible from State Highway 38. At Te Whaiti, turn off onto Minginui Road. Don't go into Minginui township, but turn right, and cross the road bridge over the Whirinaki River, then turn right onto River Road. There's a large carpark and a toilet at the road end. It's advisable to use local tourism operators who will drop you and safely store your vehicle.

Huts Central Whirinaki costs $15/night, or $7.50 for youths aged 11–17. Mangamate Hut costs $5/night, or $2.50 for youths aged 11–17. No booking is required.

Information Murupara Visitor Centre, State Highway 38, Murupara, tel: 07 366 1080, email: muruparavc@doc.govt.nz

AROUND THE MOUNTAIN CIRCUIT
EGMONT NATIONAL PARK 4–5 DAYS

Mt Taranaki dominates its hinterland like no other mountain in New Zealand. The isolated volcanic cone rises from near the Tasman Sea to reach a height of 2518 m, making it the second-highest peak in the North Island.

Trampers and climbers have long sought out the summit, or clambered around its flanks. As its name implies, the Around the Mountain Circuit completely circumnavigates Mt Taranaki, sometimes on its forested flanks, at other times emerging onto its exposed upper slopes.

The circuit involves reasonably strenuous tramping, on a track that can be rough and muddy in places. A number of streams are unbridged, and can become unfordable after heavy rain. Others can be gouged out with difficult entry and exit points. Taking in all the diversity of Egmont National Park, the circuit includes waterfalls, goblin forest, spectacular lava bluffs and, of course, many views of the mountain itself. It's a trip with multiple variations and different starting points, but is described here in the clockwise direction, beginning from the Dawson Falls Visitor Centre.

Dawson Falls to Lake Dive Hut (16 bunks, woodburner) via low-level route 3 hours, 6 km; via high-level route 4 hours, 7 km

From Dawson Falls there are two routes to Lake Dive: a lower, forested route and a higher one. The latter track climbs part way up the Fanthams Peak Track, before branching off to traverse the subalpine flanks of the peak at about the 1500 m contour. Although well poled, this section of tops is very exposed to bad weather and can be icy in winter conditions.

The Lower Lake Dive Track remains in the forest, crossing numerous small streams en route. Lake Dive is nestled in forest beside the curious mounds known as the Beehives.

Lake Dive Hut to Waiaua Gorge Hut (16 bunks, woodburner) 7–8 hours, 10 km via either route

From Lake Dive, two options – one low, one high – are again available to trampers. The high-level route retraces the Upper Lake Dive Track to the bush edge, then continues westwards along an exposed section of tops to join the Brames Falls Track, where it descends to Waiaua Gorge. It is recommended for experienced parties setting out on a good weather forecast.

The lower route descends the Auroa Track to its junction with the Taungatara Track. From here, the Auroa Track exits out at Auroa Road. Take the Taungatara Track, which sidles low on the mountain's flanks at about the 500 m contour, passing through lowland podocarp–broadleaf forest. It's a long route, with numerous streams to cross, and is often muddy. Beyond its junction with the Brames Falls Track, an aluminium ladder is used to climb out of the Waiaua Gorge to reach the nearby hut.

Waiaua Gorge Hut to Holly Hut (32 bunks, woodburner) 8–9 hours, 14 km

From Waiaua Gorge Hut, the track heads northwest, crossing a branch of the Waiaua River on a swingbridge. Pass the turnoff to the Ihaia Track (an exit route) and follow the Oaonui Track northwards to the junction with the Kahui Track. Unless you want to visit Kahui Hut (6 bunks, woodburner), the smallest and oldest hut on the circuit, continue northwards along the Kapoaiaia Track. (Trampers should note that, due to severe erosion, the Pyramid Route marked on older maps past Kahui Hut is now closed.)

The Kapoaiaia Track follows the contours of the moun-

Holly Hut, with Mt Taranaki/Egmont beyond

tain's forested slopes towards the Stony River, crossing several guts en route. After reaching the Stony River, the track – marked by cairns – continues upstream on the true left bank, crossing a few unbridged side streams en route. The Dome, a prominent lava dome flanking the Ahukawakawa Swamp, lies ahead. At the Bells Falls turnoff, it's worth dropping packs for the 30-minute return side-trip to see the voluminous waterfall. Holly Hut is a further 30 minutes away.

Holly Hut to North Egmont Summit Track junction
2–2.5 hours, 5 km
From Holly Hut, the track heads eastwards towards North Egmont, initially climbing a long series of steps, then sidling across a series of gorges. Barren volcanic landscapes dominate, with Boomerang Slip and the Dieffenbach Cliffs

prominent. There are good views of the Ahukawakawa Swamp and the Pouakai Range. Pass the Kokowai Track (another exit point) and continue ahead. At a second track junction, trampers face a decision – they can finish the track two different ways: either on the low- or high-level tracks. Both have their advantages; while the high route is shorter and offers good views, the low route passes some of the most scenic forest and waterfalls on the track.

North Egmont Summit Track junction to Dawson
Falls via high-level track 3.5–4 hours, 8 km
The high-level circuit continues around the tops, past two private huts at Tahurangi and Manganui Skifield, to The Plateau, at the end of Pembroke Road. It's an exposed route, inadvisable when the weather is bad or avalanche danger

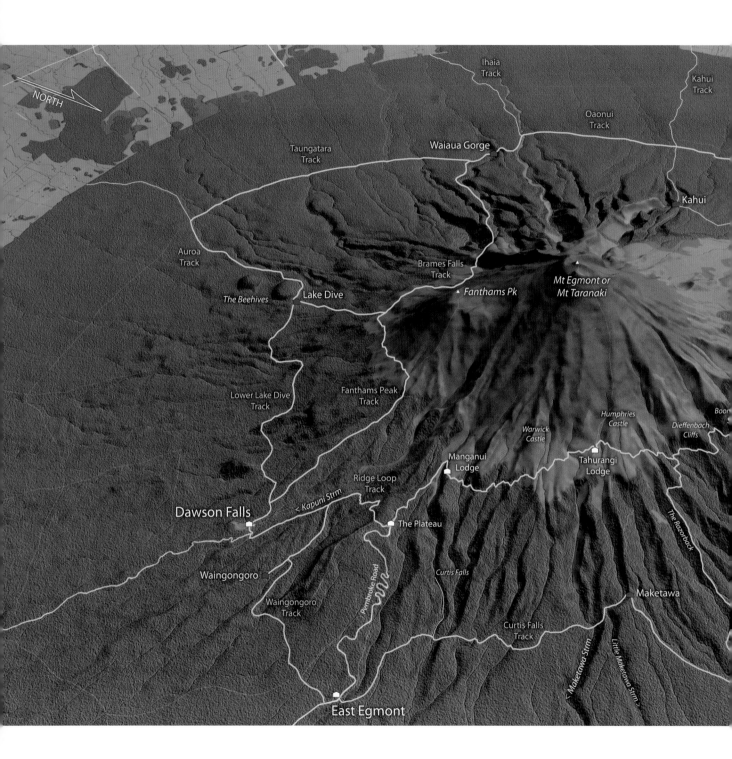

NORTH

Ihaia
Track

Kahui
Track

Oaonui
Track

Waiaua Gorge

Kahui

Taungatara
Track

Auroa
Track

Brames Falls
Track

Mt Egmont or
Mt Taranaki

The Beehives

Lake Dive

Fanthams Pk

Lower Lake Dive
Track

Fanthams Peak
Track

Humphries
Castle

Dieffenbach
Cliffs

Boor

Warwick
Castle

Manganui
Lodge

Tahurangi
Lodge

Ridge Loop
Track

Dawson Falls

< Kapuni Strm

The Plateau

The Razorback

Waingongoro

Curtis Falls

Maketawa

Waingongoro
Track

Pembroke Road

Curtis Falls
Track

< Maketawa Strm

Little Maketawa Strm >

East Egmont

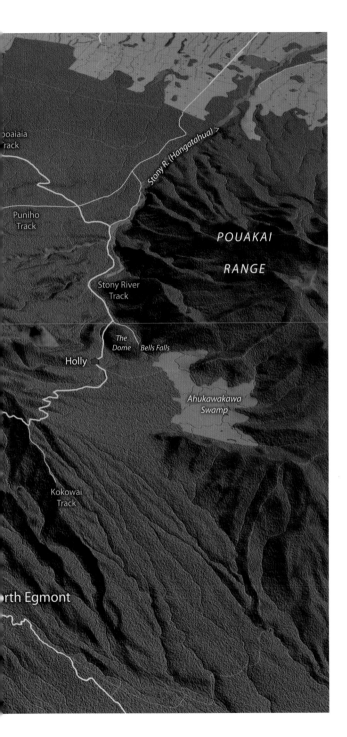

exists. During good weather, however, it offers excellent views of Humphries and Warwick castles, as well as the east Taranaki farmlands. From The Plateau, pick up a series of tracks leading back to Dawson Falls.

North Egmont Summit Track junction to Dawson Falls via low-level track and Maketawa Hut
6–7 hours, 13 km

From the track junction, head left onto a descent along The Razorback, which leads down into forest and the North Egmont Visitor Centre. From the visitor centre, pick up the track to Maketawa Hut (16 bunks, woodburner), which takes about an hour. Beyond Maketawa, the track crosses the Little Maketawa and Maketawa streams in quick succession, passes the Curtis Falls, and continues to the toilets and shelter at East Egmont, on Pembroke Road. From here, the Waingongoro Track sidles through goblin forest to reach a swingbridge over the Waingongoro River. Waingongoro Hut (16 bunks, woodburner) can be visited on a short side-track. Otherwise, continue along the Waingongoro Track, which climbs steadily before reaching the junction with the Ridge Loop Track. Descend this track to a bridge across the Kapuni Stream and then walk up the road to the Dawson Falls Visitor Centre. While walking up the road it's worth looking at the historic and still operative Dawson Falls hydroelectric power station, which provides power to the tourist lodge.

Grade Medium–hard
Map Topo50 BJ29 Mount Taranaki or Mount Egmont
Access From Eltham, on State Highway 3, turn onto Eltham Road to reach Kaponga. Turn right here onto Manaia Road. At the road end is the Dawson Falls Visitor Centre, with information, toilets and an intentions book.
Huts All huts cost $15/night, or $7.50 for youths aged 11–17, except for Kahui Hut, which costs $5/night, or $2.50 for youths. No booking is required.
Information Dawson Falls Visitor Centre, Manaia Road, tel: 027 443 0248. Taranaki/Egmont National Park Visitor Centre (North Egmont), Egmont Road, Inglewood, tel: 06 756 0990, email: egmontvc@doc.govt.nz

TONGARIRO NORTHERN CIRCUIT
TONGARIRO NATIONAL PARK 3–4 DAYS

Tongariro is by far the most popular national park in the North Island, attracting hundreds of thousands of skiers, walkers and trampers every year. The park centres around three active volcanoes: Tongariro, Ngauruhoe and Ruapehu, all of which are considered sacred by Maori. In 1887, Horonuku Te Heuheu Tukino IV, chief of the local Ngati Tuwharetoa iwi, gifted the peaks to the government as the basis for the country's first national park. The mountains continue to play an important spiritual role for both Tuwharetoa and another iwi, Ngati Rangi. In recognition of their strong spiritual links to the volcanoes, in 1993 the park became the first to receive joint UNESCO World Heritage Status for both its landscape and cultural values.

Needless to say, many multi-day tramps in the park are possible, with the Tongariro Northern Circuit a popular choice. One of the eight Great Walks, the track crosses some of the most colourful and remarkable volcanic topography anywhere on the planet, with expansive views and good huts. Be warned, however, that part of the track overlaps with the Tongariro Alpine Crossing, the most popular day tramp in New Zealand. On this section you will likely meet a steady stream of people, and it's far from a 'wilderness' experience.

The circuit is exposed to the weather no matter which direction it comes from, a fact that has led to deaths for those who are ill-equipped. You'll need to take warm and weatherproof clothing as the weather can change with lethal speed. In winter, skills with an ice axe and crampons may be necessary too.

Volcanic hazards also pose risks. When the Te Maari craters erupted twice in 2012, Ketetahi Hut (previously a popular destination for those tramping the circuit) was damaged beyond repair. The explosion catapulted boulders into the hut, which was fortunately empty at the time.

Whakapapa Village to new Waihohonu Hut (29 bunks, woodburner) 5–6 hours, 14 km
The track begins from Ngauruhoe Place, 100 m from the Tongariro National Park Visitor Centre. Two options – the upper and lower tracks – lead to the spectacular Taranaki Falls; either takes about an hour. From the falls, a further two hours' tramp crosses exposed terrain to Tama Saddle – the low point between Mts Ngauruhoe and Ruapehu. From Tama Saddle, it is possible to take a short side-trip to visit the nearby Tama Lakes (30 to 90 minutes return). Past Tama Saddle, a further two to three hours' tramping beside the Waihohonu Stream leads to the Waihohonu Hut, passing en route the side-track to the historic Old Waihohonu Hut (built 1903–04).

Waihohonu Hut to Oturere Hut (26 bunks) 3 hours, 8.5 km
After leaving Waihohonu Hut, the track climbs a ridge and then crosses a beech-clad valley. Beyond, the track traverses barren, undulating terrain, with good views of the imposing Mt Ngauruhoe, which can also be enjoyed from Oturere Hut.

Oturere Hut to Emerald Lakes 1.5–2 hours, 3 km
An endless variety of jagged lava flows characterise the Oturere Valley, created from various Red Crater eruptions between 2500 and 87,000 years ago, making it a surreal place to walk through on a misty day. Near the end of the valley, the track begins a steep climb up to the lip of Central

Mt Ngauruhoe from the Tongariro Northern Circuit

Crater, right beside the Emerald Lakes. These are three old explosion pits, now filled by highly acidic lakes, all of an arresting blue-green colour that changes hue according to the light and time of day.

Emerald Lakes to Mangatepopo Hut (23 bunks) 3–4 hours, 7 km

From the Emerald Lakes, pass the turnoff to Blue Lake and Ketetahi Shelter, and begin the climb up the scoria slopes of the colourful Red Crater. Loose rock can make this a tough climb. Above Red Crater, at the highest point on the circuit (Pt 1886 m) is an outstanding viewpoint. Ngauruhoe rises starkly from South Crater, with Ruapehu partially hidden behind. A poled side-trail leads to the summit of Tongariro (1967 m), lowest of the three major peaks in the park. From here, there is a steady descent along a ridge to South Crater. Poles lead across the flat expanse of the crater, ending on a lip overlooking the Mangatepopo Valley.

From the lip, there's the option of climbing Ngauruhoe (2287 m), an energy-sapping but rewarding scramble up steep scree slopes. Otherwise, head downhill on a series of sharp zigzags that end beside the babbling Mangatepopo Stream. Old lava flows originating from Mt Ngauruhoe dominate the valley. There are toilets near the Soda Springs. Mangatepopo Hut lies just 20 minutes from the end of Mangatepopo Road.

Mangatepopo Hut to Whakapapa Village
3–5 hours, 8.5 km

Many people choose to end their tramp at Mangatepopo, and do not complete the full circuit back to Whakapapa Village using this track, which is eroded in places and crosses several streams. After leaving Mangatepopo Hut, head towards the Mangatepopo Road. The track to Whakapapa Village branches off after five minutes. Initially, the track rounds the western slopes of Pukekaikiore (1692 m), thought to be one of the older vents of the Tongariro complex, then passes Pukeonake (1225 m), a low scoria cone. Views of Mt Ruapehu open up as you approach Whakapapa Village.

Grade Easy–medium

Maps Topo50 BH35 Turangi, BH34 Mount Ruapehu, BJ35 Waiouru

Access Whakapapa Village is located on State Highway 48, which branches off State Highway 47 between Turangi and National Park. It has accommodation, toilets, cafés, a shop and the Tongariro National Park Visitor Centre, which is well worth a visit. Operators based at Whakapapa Village and Turangi can arrange transport to shorten the trip.

Huts and campsites These must be booked in advance in the peak summer season (October to April). Huts cost $32/night, and are free for youths aged under 18. The campsites (one near each hut) cost $15/night. Huts have gas heating and cooking facilities during the peak summer season, but trampers must carry their own stoves for the remainder of the year.

Information and booking Book huts online at: tel: 0800 NZ GREAT WALKS (0800 694732), email: greatwalks bookings@doc.govt.nz, website: www.greatwalks.co.nz Tongariro National Park Visitor Centre, Whakapapa Village, tel: 07 892 3729, email: tongarirovc@doc.govt.nz

Lake Rotoaira

46

Ketetahi Shelter

Blue Lake

Tongariro

Emerald
Lakes

pt 1886

Red
Crater

Soda
Springs

< Mangatepopo Strm

South Crater

Oturere Valley

Mangatepopo

Mangatepopo
road end

Pukekaikiore

Ngauruhoe

Oturere

Upper Tama

Lower Tama

Waihohonu Strm >

Tama
Saddle

Old Waihohonu
(historic)

Waihohonu

to
Desert Road
(SH1)

Around Ruapehu
Track

RUAPEHU ROUND THE MOUNTAIN TRACK
TONGARIRO NATIONAL PARK 4–6 DAYS

The Ruapehu Round the Mountain Track lies in the southern half of the World Heritage Tongariro National Park. It circumnavigates Mt Ruapehu, which at 2797 m is the highest peak in the North Island, and the highest volcano in New Zealand. En route, the track ranges through a striking diversity of landscapes, including beech-clad valleys, alpine herbfields, rough scoria slopes, waterfalls and the stark Rangipo Desert. While the Tongariro Northern Circuit (see page 120) continues to attract people in droves, the Ruapehu Round the Mountain Track usually offers a quieter alternative. However, expect it to be busy where the track overlaps the Tongariro Northern Circuit between Whakapapa Village and Waihohonu Hut.

Ruapehu, of course, dominates views for the entire trip, its appearance changing according to the angle. The eastern side of the track also offers good views of the neighbouring Kaimanawa Ranges, while on the west the rugged terrain around the headwaters of the Whanganui River can be seen.

Trampers need to be aware that Mt Ruapehu can erupt with little warning, and should always check with DOC before departing on their trip. The track crosses several known lahar paths; these large flows of volcanic ash and mud can sweep down the mountainside at speeds of up to 50 kph. Even when volcanic activity remains subdued, many sections of the track are exposed to the wind and weather, and lack shelter for long periods. While there are no major alpine passes, the track reaches almost 1600 m and during winter trampers need to carry full alpine gear. Walking the track in either direction is equally enjoyable. The clockwise direction, starting from Whakapapa Village, is described here. For those who don't wish to complete the whole circuit, various options for shorter trips are easily planned, as the track crosses three roads en route.

Whakapapa Village to Waihohonu Hut (29 bunks, woodburner) 5–6 hours, 14 km

The track begins from Ngauruhoe Place, 100 m from the Tongariro National Park Visitor Centre. Two options – the upper and lower tracks – lead to the spectacular Taranaki Falls; either takes about an hour. From the falls, a further two hours' tramp crosses exposed terrain to Tama Saddle – the low point between Mts Ngauruhoe and Ruapehu. From Tama Saddle, it is possible to take a short side-trip to visit the nearby Tama Lakes (30 to 90 minutes return). Past Tama Saddle, a further two to three hours' tramping beside the Waihohonu Stream leads to the Waihohonu Hut, passing en route the side-track to the historic Old Waihohonu Hut (built 1903–04).

Waihohonu Hut to Rangipo Hut (20 bunks, woodburner) 5 hours, 12.5 km

This part of the track crosses the only true desert landscape in New Zealand, featuring wind-sculpted sand, volcanic rock and scant vegetation. After passing the Ohinepango Springs, the track traverses the eastern side of Mt Ruapehu, crosses the Tukino Mountain Road and continues to the Whangaehu River. When Ruapehu erupted in 1995, a lahar destroyed a footbridge over the Whangaehu, which has since been rebuilt. Trampers should not dawdle or stop while crossing the Whangaehu Valley.

Beyond the Whangaehu River, it is a further 40 minutes to Rangipo Hut, situated at 1560 m. While it can be a bleak spot in bad weather, on a fine day the hut has

Trampers on the boardwalk beside Lake Rotokawa

magnificent views over the surrounding desert and the Kaimanawa Ranges.

Rangipo Hut to Mangaehuehu Hut (18 bunks, woodburner) 5–6 hours, 8.5 km

On this section, an undulating traverse takes you from the Rangipo Desert, across the impressive Waihianoa Gorge, and through copses of mountain beech forest on the southern flanks of Mt Ruapehu to Mangaehuehu Hut. From this angle, Ruapehu's shape is dominated by the pyramid of Girdlestone Peak, the southernmost of the volcano's several summits.

Mangaehuehu Hut to Mangaturuturu Hut (10 bunks, woodburner) 4.5–5 hours, 12 km

From Mangaehuehu Hut, the track leads through a mixture of tussocklands and beech stands to a signposted turnoff indicating a possible side-trip to

Blyth Hut (60 minutes return). The main Ruapehu Round the Mountain Track continues, passing the sizeable Waitonga Falls (39 m), and further on crossing alpine wetlands beside Lake Rotokawa on a boardwalk. Another track junction indicates the Old Blyth Track. Continue on the main track, which soon emerges onto the Ohakune Mountain Road. Here, a 3 km walk up the road leads to a signpost at Wanganui Corner, where the track resumes. This next spectacular section crosses alpine herbfields and descends a lava ridge past the creamy-coloured 'Cascades' to Mangaturuturu Hut. Built in 1958 by the Wanganui Tramping Club, the hut has a spectacular view of Ruapehu through its front window.

Mangaturuturu Hut to Whakapapaiti Hut (18 bunks, woodburner) 5–6 hours, 10 km

After crossing the Mangaturuturu River (which can be impassable in flood), the track climbs to picturesque Lake

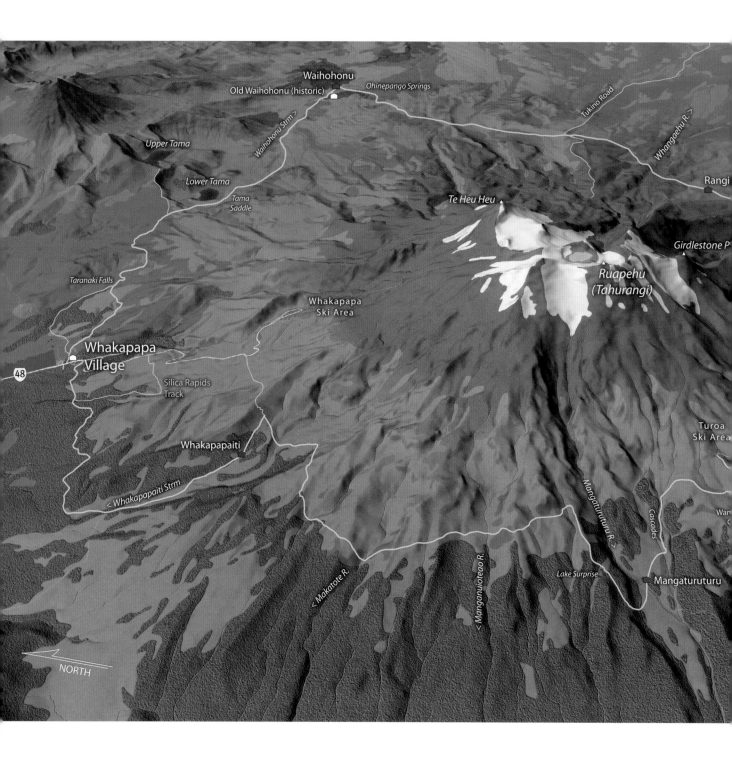

Waihohonu

Old Waihohonu (historic)

Ohinepango Springs

Tukino Road

Whangaehu R.

Upper Tama

Waihohonu Strm >

Lower Tama

Tama Saddle

Rangi

Te Heu Heu

Girdlestone P

Taranaki Falls

Whakapapa Ski Area

Ruapehu (Tahurangi)

Whakapapa Village

48

Silica Rapids Track

Whakapapaiti

Turoa Ski Area

< *Whakapapaiti Strm*

Manganuioteao R.

Mangaturuturu R. >

Cascades

Wai

< *Makatote R.*

Lake Surprise

Mangaturuturu

NORTH

Surprise, and beyond up a series of steps to the ridge above. Unfolding are excellent views of Hauhangatahi (1521 m), an extinct volcano lying to the west.

The track traverses the exposed western flanks of Mt Ruapehu, across the Manganui o te Ao and Makatote rivers, and finally enters the Whakapapaiti Valley. A track junction here indicates two options to finish the tramp. The shortest route avoids Whakapapaiti Hut altogether and leads to Bruce Road, taking 30–40 minutes. The alternative option is descend downstream for 20 minutes to Whakapapaiti Hut and carry on from there.

Whakapapaiti Hut to Whakapapa Village
2.5–3 hours, 9 km

From the hut, the track leads through forest down the Whakapapaiti Valley, crossing the river twice (which can be impassable in flood), before swinging east towards Whakapapa Village. The final two hours leads through beech forest interspersed with cabbage trees and pahautea, and joins the Silica Rapids Track to end at Whakapapa Village.

Grade Medium
Maps Topo50 BJ34 Mount Ruapehu, BJ35 Waiouru
Access Whakapapa Village is located on State Highway 48, which branches off State Highway 47 between Turangi and National Park. It has accommodation, toilets, cafés, a shop and the Tongariro National Park Visitor Centre, which is well worth a visit.
Huts Rangipo, Mangaehuehu, Mangaturuturu and Whakapapaiti huts cost $15/night, or $7.50 for youths aged 11–17. No booking is required. Waihohonu Hut is part of the Tongariro Northern Circuit Great Walk, and during the peak season (October to April) must be booked in advance. It costs $32/night, and is free for youths aged under 18.
Information and booking Book huts online at: tel: 0800 NZ GREAT WALKS (0800 694732), email: great walksbooking@doc.govt.nz, website: www.doc.govt.nz Tongariro National Park Visitor Centre, Whakapapa Village, tel: 07 892 3729, email: tongarirovc@doc.govt.nz

WAIPAKIHI HUT
KAIMANAWA FOREST PARK 3 DAYS

It is perhaps inevitable that the volcanic attractions of adjacent Tongariro National Park overshadow the good tramping available in the Kaimanawa Range. Those making the effort, however, will find much to interest them in Kaimanawa Forest Park, as well as being able to enjoy some of the finest views of the neighbouring volcanoes.

One of the best overnight trips in the park is the tramp over the Umukarikari Range to Waipakihi Hut. The second day involves an amble down the Waipakihi River to an excellent campsite at the base of the Urchin Track. From the Urchin tops, two options exist: a descent and the walk along the road back to your vehicle, or a link track that leads back to the Umukarikari Range. Altogether, this tramp makes the ideal introduction to Kaimanawa tramping, and forms one of the park's few round trips that can be accomplished in a weekend.

Kaimanawa Road to Waipakihi Hut (12 bunks, woodburner) via Umukarikari Range
4–6 hours, 15 km

From the Umukarikari Track carpark, the route meanders gently for 15 minutes before beginning a steady climb up a beech-covered spur that leads towards the tops. At the bushline, the track emerges onto a narrow ridge, which soon enough opens onto expansive, rolling tops.

While subalpine plants exist in patches, the Umukarikari Range is typical of many broad Kaimanawa tops, with scant vegetation and no tarns. The route, marked by poles, continues over Sharp Cone and reaches its high point a short distance on at Umukarikari itself (1591 m). From here, the views span across virtually the entire Volcanic Plateau, with Mts Ruapehu and Ngauruhoe prominent.

Beyond Umukarikari, a long section of undulating travel leads along tops, eventually dropping into the head of the Waipakihi Valley. A small tributary of the Waipakihi is crossed shortly before the final short plod up to Waipakihi Hut. Plenty of campsites exist around the hut.

Waipakihi Hut to Urchin Track via Waipakihi River
3–4.5 hours, 11 km

The Waipakihi River boasts extensive river flats, interspersed with beech-fringed riverbanks. There is no defined track, and the route downstream is simply a matter of crossing at will to whatever bank seems easiest. If the river level is up, it may be best to wait at Waipakihi Hut, although it is possible to stay on the true right bank the whole way. There are numerous places to camp en route, although a particularly well-used site lies tucked into the beech forest at the base of the track leading to Urchin (which is signposted).

Urchin Track to Kaimanawa Road 3 hours, 7 km

The Urchin Track doesn't muck around – it's a quick, steep 300 m climb onto the 3 km section of tops across Urchin (1392 m), marked by poles. As well as more views westwards towards the volcanoes, there are princely vistas of the Waipakihi Valley and the jumbled ridges of the Kaimanawa Range. On the far side of Urchin, a steady descent through forest ends at another branch of Kaimanawa Road.

Urchin to Kaimanawa Road via link track to Umukarikari Range, 5 hours, 13 km

Alternatively, from the Urchin tops, there is now a link track that follows a forested ridge back to the Umukarikari Range, joining it near Sharp Cone. Then it's a simple matter of retracing your inward route back to the carpark.

Opposite *Waipakihi River*

Grade Medium–hard

Maps Topo50 BH36 Motutere

Access On State Highway 1, some 15 km south of Turangi, turn onto Kaimanawa Road. After 4 km, turn left onto a side road marked with a sign to the Umukarikari Track; this immediately crosses a bridge. After 500 m, turn right and follow this road to the end, where there is space to park near the signposted track start. As the Urchin Track ends on another road 5 km away, using this track to finish will either require some road walking or a car shuffle.

Hut and camping Waipakihi Hut costs $5/night, or $2.50 for youths aged 11–17. No booking is required. Three roadside campsites exist, at Urchin, Kaimanawa Road and Waikoko.

Information DOC Turangi, 69 The Mall, Turangi, tel: 07 384 7106, email: turangi@doc.govt.nz

RANGIWAHIA HUT
RUAHINE FOREST PARK 1–2 DAYS

Rangiwahia Hut, or Rangi as local trampers often refer to it, offers Manawatu trampers what Sunrise Hut (see page 134) offers those in Hawke's Bay: a large, comfortable hut set on the tops, with good views and accessible via a relatively easy track.

Rangiwahia, however, occupies a position on the western side of the Ruahine Range, where the vegetation is very different to that on the east. While beech dominates the forests of the east, the western forests are more diverse; in addition to beech, they contain podocarps and broadleaf species, with the conical mountain cedar, or pahautea, forming a distinctive band near the bushline. When winter snows cover the tops and forest, the Rangiwahia Track is a delight. The route is well benched, and has been recently upgraded to avoid a slip.

Renfrew Road to Rangiwahia Hut (13 bunks, woodburner) 2–2.5 hours, 4 km

From the Renfrew Road carpark, a well-graded track leads upwards through dense forest, with the occasional mountain cabbage tree arching attractively overhead. A new section of track zigzags steadily upwards, with wooden steps in places, to where it offers a view of the arched bridge that spans an impressive chasm some 70 m above a tributary of the Mangawharariki Stream. After crossing the bridge, the track begins a steady climb through pahautea forest and into subalpine shrublands.

Rangiwahia Hut at dawn

Shortly before emerging above the bushline, the track crosses a narrow stream beneath a small waterfall. Rangiwahia Hut sits perched on the tops, overlooking the Rangitikei region and the distant mountains of Tongariro National Park. The current Rangiwahia Hut, built in 1983–84, is the third one on the site. For a while in the 1930s and 1940s, the slopes behind the original Rangiwahia Hut attracted skiers, who installed a rope tow powered by the engine from an Indian motorbike. These days the snows are too unreliable for consistent skiing, although after a heavy dump the area offers good terrain for ski-touring.

In memory of the hut's history, old skis have been attached to the hut exterior, and a modern touch is the delightful scenes of local birds and bush painted on the woodshed and toilets by local Mangaweka artist Julie Oliver.

Rangiwahia Hut to Renfrew Road via Deadmans Track 4–5 hours, 10 km

Past the hut, a gentle 3 km stroll leads up the well-rutted and poled tussock ridge towards Mangahuia (1580 m), one of the high points on the Whanahuia Range. On a good day, the open tops offer excellent views of the main Ruahine Range and the headwaters of the Oroua River. Far to the west, the lonely summit of Mt Taranaki can sometimes be seen. From Mangahuia, the Deadmans Track (marked by poles) provides an alternative option to tramp back to the road end, following an adjacent ridge.

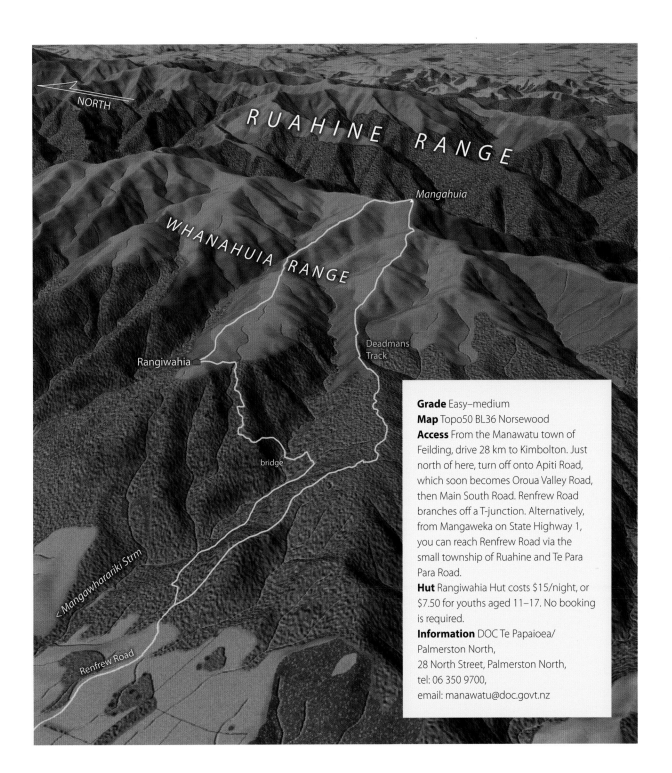

NORTH

RUAHINE RANGE

WHANAHUIA RANGE

Mangahuia

Deadmans Track

Rangiwahia

bridge

< Mangawharariki Strm

Renfrew Road

Grade Easy–medium
Map Topo50 BL36 Norsewood
Access From the Manawatu town of
Feilding, drive 28 km to Kimbolton. Just
north of here, turn off onto Apiti Road,
which soon becomes Oroua Valley Road,
then Main South Road. Renfrew Road
branches off a T-junction. Alternatively,
from Mangaweka on State Highway 1,
you can reach Renfrew Road via the
small township of Ruahine and Te Para
Para Road.
Hut Rangiwahia Hut costs $15/night, or
$7.50 for youths aged 11–17. No booking
is required.
Information DOC Te Papaioea/
Palmerston North,
28 North Street, Palmerston North,
tel: 06 350 9700,
email: manawatu@doc.govt.nz

TE PUIA LODGE
KAWEKA FOREST PARK 1–2 DAYS

The largest and most popular hut in Kaweka Forest Park, Te Puia Lodge is a worthy destination for families or those with limited tramping experience. Best of all, the hut lies within easy reach of some very pleasant hot springs. No other tramp in New Zealand offers the chance to enjoy a soak at the beginning, middle and end of your trip!

The Gums carpark to Mangatutu Hot Springs
10 minutes, 500 m

The first soak of the day begins before you even shoulder your pack. From the camping area at The Gums, a five-minute walk leads down to the Mangatutu Hot Springs, which issue steam from slopes above the Mohaka River. A pipe diverts hot water from the stream into two tubs, with room for up to 10 people. (Note: keep your head above water to prevent any chance of contracting amoebic meningoencephalitis.)

The Gums carpark to Te Puia Lodge (26 bunks)
2–2.5 hours, 7 km

After initially sidling around bush-covered slopes, crossing two side streams en route, the Te Puia Track descends onto a manuka-fringed flat near the Mohaka River, which offers good places to swim. The Mohaka, one of the principal rivers draining the Kaweka Range, is well known for its good trout fishing and excellent rafting. Considering the rather precipitous nature of the valley, the track is surprisingly easy, with only a few climbs to avoid bluffs. Manuka dominates the forest, which is regenerating after past fires, but at about the halfway mark the track passes through the first section of mature beech forest. Situated on a pleasant flat near the middle reaches of the Mohaka River, Te Puia Lodge offers bunk space for 26 in two separate rooms.

Opposite *The Mohaka River from the Te Puia Track*

Te Puia Lodge to Mangatainoka Hot Springs,
40 minutes, 2.5 km each way

From the lodge, head up the valley and cross the swingbridge over the Makino River. Undulating travel through beech forest leads to an appealing terrace beside the Mohaka River, where there is a good camping area beside the hot springs, located among podocarp trees. The springs issue from a bank into two fibreglass tubs; their temperatures can be adjusted using water scoops. After an evening's soak, the following day involves a leisurely return back along the track to the carpark, where the Mangatutu Hot Springs await.

Grade Easy
Maps Topo50 BH37 Rangitaiki, BJ37 Kuripapango
Access From Napier, it is a 75 km drive to the track start. Follow Puketitiri Road for 36 km before turning right into Pakaututu Road, then follow this for 9 km before turning left into Makahu Road. This winding gravel road crosses a ford (which may be impassable after rain) and ends at The Gums carpark.
Hut and camping Te Puia Lodge costs $15/night, or $7.50 for youths aged 11–17. No booking is required. It has gas-heating facilities, but trampers must carry their own stove for cooking. Campsites exist at The Gums road end, near Te Puia Lodge and beside the Mangatainoka Hot Springs.
Information DOC Ahuriri/Napier, 59 Marine Parade, Napier, tel: 06 834 3111, email: napier@doc.govt.nz

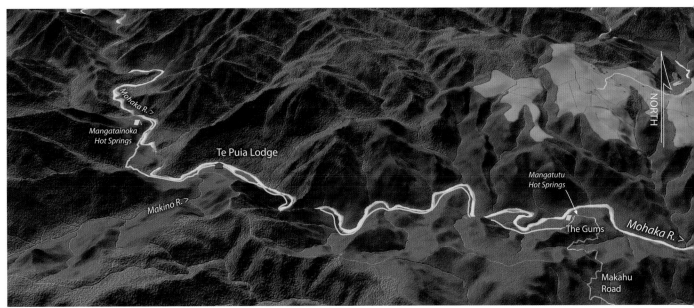

Mohaka R. >

Mangatainoka
Hot Springs

Te Puia Lodge

Makino R. >

NORTH

Mangatutu
Hot Springs

The Gums

Mohaka R. >

Makahu
Road

SUNRISE HUT
RUAHINE FOREST PARK 1–2 DAYS

Sunrise Hut occupies a charming subalpine basin in the Ruahine Range, overlooking the hill country and distant coastline of Hawke's Bay. A short climb from the hut leads to Armstrong Saddle, an expansive tussock flat where, on a good day, the distant volcanoes of Ruapehu and Ngauruhoe are visible.

Although it is a reasonable climb up through forest to the hut, the high-quality, well-graded track ensures Sunrise is a destination suitable for trampers of all abilities, including families with young children.

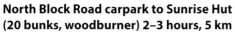

North Block Road carpark to Sunrise Hut (20 bunks, woodburner) 2–3 hours, 5 km

From the carpark, the Sunrise Track leads across farmland to the bush edge. A stile across a fence leads into a section of tall podocarp forest, one of the best remaining examples of its type left on the flanks of the Ruahine Range. Unless you want to visit Triplex Hut on the Swamp Track, follow the signs indicating Sunrise Hut. At the end of the podocarp forest, the Sunrise Track begins to climb, zigzagging up a forested ridge. After two to three hours of moderate ascent, you emerge above the bushline. Sunrise Hut is nearby, set among subalpine plants and a patch of stunted forest in Buttercup Hollow. Two hardened sites provide space for campers.

If the weather proves favourable, a stroll to Armstrong Saddle is worth the effort. Beginning behind the hut, the track passes through stunted forest before skirting one of the most impressive erosion scars in the Ruahine Range. Beyond, a gentle climb leads to Armstrong Saddle (1369 m). It is named after pioneer aviator Hamish Armstrong, who crashed here in 1935. Armstrong survived the crash and presumably attempted to walk out, but searchers never found his body.

Sunrise Hut to carpark via Triplex Hut and Swamp Track 2.5–3 hours, 6 km

Halfway back down the Sunrise Track, a trail branches off south to Waipawa Forks Hut, providing an alternative route back to your vehicle (note: this requires following the Waipawa River, which can be impassable when it is in flood). However, most parties continue to Triplex Hut, followed by a walk along the Swamp Track back to the carpark.

Armstrong Saddle with Mt Ruapehu beyond

Mangaweka

RUAHINE RANGE

Te Atuaoparapara

Waipawa
Saddle

Armstrong
Saddle

Sunrise

Buttercup
Hollow

Waipawa Forks

< Waipawa R.

< Triplex Ck

Swamp Track

Triplex

North Block Road
carpark

NORTH

Grade Easy
Map Topo50 BK36 Toaroa Junction
Access From Napier, follow State Highway 50 for 66 km, then turn left onto Wakarara Road. After 20 km, turn left onto North Block Road, following this to the carpark at the road end. The total driving distance from Napier is 100 km.

Huts Sunrise Hut costs $15/night, or $7.50 for youths aged 11–17. Triplex and Waipawa Forks huts both cost $5/night, or $2.50 for youths. No booking is required.
Information DOC Ahuriri/Napier, 59 Marine Parade, Napier, tel: 06 834 3111, email: napier@doc.govt.nz

SOUTHERN CROSSING
TARARUA FOREST PARK 3 DAYS

The Southern Crossing of the Tararua Range is a track with a long history, dating back to the early part of the twentieth century. Two groups, one based in Otaki and the other in Greytown, wanted their respective regions connected by a track crossing the range via Mt Hector. Through their efforts, the track was cut and three huts were erected, one near Otaki Forks, another at Alpha and the third in the Tauherenikau Valley. Later work in the 1920s by the newly formed Tararua Tramping Club saw further huts erected at Kime and Field.

Beginning at Otaki Forks, the 44 km track ascends through forest to Field Hut, then onto the tops to reach Kime Hut. From Kime, it climbs Mt Hector, the highest point in the southern Tararua Range, and one that affords 360-degree views over Wellington and the Wairarapa. South of Mt Hector, the route crosses a series of other subalpine peaks, reaching the bushline near Alpha Hut.

From Alpha Hut, the original Southern Crossing route used to descend to the Tauherenikau Valley, then climb over Mt Reeves to end at Walls Whare, near Greytown. These days, however, most parties opt to walk out to Kaitoke, near Upper Hutt. Although it is undoubtedly easier to organise transport for this route, it's somewhat ironic that it remains in the west without actually crossing the range.

Otaki Forks to Field Hut (20 bunks, woodburner) 2.5–3 hours, 8 km

Otaki Forks is a popular place for picnicking, swimming and camping. From the overnight parking area, a short track leads down to a picnic area and a footbridge over the Waiotauru River. Across the bridge, past the turnoff to Parawai Lodge, a brief climb leads to a grassy terrace. At a track junction follow the signposted track leading to Field Hut. A long but not particularly strenuous ascent through forest ensues to reach the historic hut – built in 1924 and now the oldest purpose-built tramping club hut remaining in the country.

Field Hut to Kime Hut (20 bunks) 2–3 hours, 6 km

Above Field Hut, a short section in forest and subalpine shrubs leads to Table Top (1047 m). Beyond here, the track ascends the open tops of Judd Ridge, which can be very exposed to the elements. While there are few marker poles, the track is worn enough for it to remain clear except when it's obscured by snow. Near the top, some waratahs appear,

and shortly after comes the signpost indicating the turnoff to Bridge Peak and Maungahuka Hut. Not far from here, just over the rise of Hut Mound (1440 m), Kime Hut lies nestled in a shallow dip by a prominent tarn.

Kime Hut to Alpha Hut (20 bunks, woodburner) 4–5 hours, 10 km

From Kime Hut, you embark across the exposed tops to Alpha Hut. Initially, the track climbs to Field Peak (1483 m), then drops sharply to a saddle, from where the final ascent to Mt Hector begins. At 1529 m, Mt Hector is the highest point on the crossing, and one of the finest viewpoints in the Tararua Range. A large wooden cross marks its unmistakable summit. On a good day the Kaikoura Ranges can be seen, rising beyond Wellington Harbour, while Kapiti Island and the Marlborough Sounds lie to the west.

From Mt Hector, the route heads almost directly south, dropping to a shallow saddle before climbing over The Beehives (1485 m). Beyond is a narrow section of ridge that

can be unnerving in high winds. Undulating tops travel leads to Atkinson (1472 m). Past Pt 1372 m, the terrain remains flat as far as Aston (1376 m), where the track curls southeast around the Dress Circle. After a climb onto Alpha (1361 m), the track swings directly east. Alpha Hut lies down the other side, nestled among stunted silver beech trees.

Alpha Hut to Kaitoke via Tauherenikau and Smith Creek 7–9 hours, 20 km

From Alpha Hut, a forested track leads to the descent into Hells Gate, followed by a stiff climb up the far side. Beyond, at a track junction, the Bull Mound Track branches off towards the Tauherenikau Valley, as does another on the summit of Omega (1118 m). Continue south along the undulating forested terrain of Marchant Ridge.

While passing through attractive silver beech forest, the Marchant Ridge Track is deceptively arduous, and a longer but preferable alternative lies on the route out through the Tauherenikau Valley via the Block XVI Track (which is clearly signposted on Marchant Ridge). Although this involves a 300 m descent, travel is generally flat once you are down in the Tauherenikau Valley, and crosses forested terraces on the river's true right (one exception is a climb around Blue Slip). At Smith Creek Shelter, a well-benched track ascends steadily to the head of Smith Creek, interrupted by one detour around a slip (surefooted trampers can work their way around the base of the slip). Near the head of Smith Creek, the track climbs through regenerating forest over Puffer Saddle to begin a sidle towards Kaitoke, passing the Marchant Ridge Track en route.

Above *Trampers crossing Table Top*

Top *Hut Mound, Southern Crossing Track*
Above *Tramper in mist on Judd Ridge*

Grade Hard
Map Topo50 BP33 Featherston
Access From State Highway 1, just south of Otaki, turn onto Otaki Gorge Road, which winds its way for 19 km into Tararua Forest Park. Park in the overnight carpark, near the caretaker's residence. At the Kaitoke end, DOC have recently established a new carpark on Kiwi Ranch Road, which branches off Marchant Road 2 km from State Highway 2.
Huts All huts cost $5/night, or $2.50 for youths aged 11–17. No booking is required.
Information DOC Poneke/Wellington Visitor Centre, 18 Manners Street, Wellington, tel: 04 384 7770, email: wellington@doc.govt.nz
DOC Whakaoriori/Masterton, 220 South Road, Masterton, tel: 06 377 0700, email: masterton@doc.govt.nz

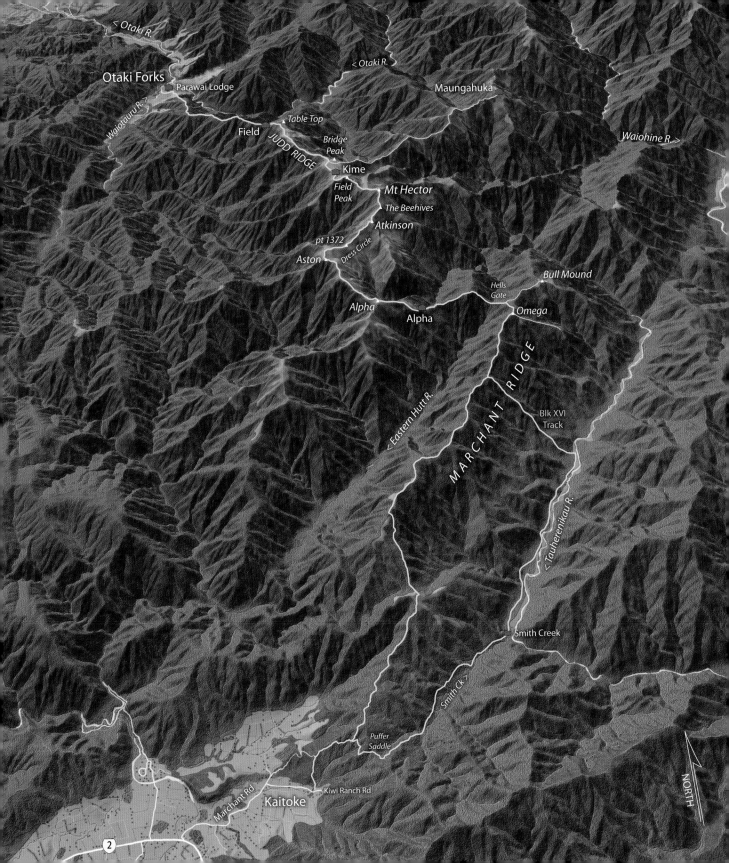

< Otaki R.

< Otaki R.

Otaki Forks   Parawai Lodge

Maungahuka

Waiotauru R. >

Field   JUDD RIDGE   Table Top

Waiohine R. >

Bridge
Peak

Kime

Field
Peak

Mt Hector

The Beehives

Atkinson

pt 1372

Aston   Dress Circle

Alpha

Alpha

Hells
Gate

Bull Mound

Omega

< Eastern Hutt R.

M A R C H A N T   R I D G E

Blk XVI
Track

< Tauherenikau R.

Smith Creek

Smith Ck >

Puffer
Saddle

Marchant Rd   Kiwi Ranch Rd

Kaitoke

NORTH

2

MT HOLDSWORTH–JUMBO CIRCUIT
TARARUA FOREST PARK 2 DAYS

Ever since the Mount Holdsworth Track Committee built the first Mountain House hut and began to promote the area in 1907, this tramp has enjoyed increasing popularity. With two huts perched on the bush edge, both offering fine views, and one set in the forest of the Atiwhakatu Valley, this two-day round trip has become something of a Tararua classic. While the tracks are well graded and well maintained, and are suitable for the average tramper, the section along the tops still requires care, particularly in high winds or low visibility. The trip can be walked either way, but is described here in the clockwise direction.

Mt Holdsworth Road to Powell Hut (28 bunks, gas cookers, woodburner) 3.5–4 hours, 7 km

From the carpark, follow a gravelled track up the valley, making sure you stop at Holdsworth Lodge to sign the intentions book. Shortly beyond, the track crosses the Atiwhakatu River on a footbridge. After 10–15 minutes' walk, the track forks; head left up the well-benched and gravelled Gentle Annie Track, which climbs steadily through mixed beech–hardwood–podocarp forest. A platform at Rocky Lookout, accessible on a side-track, provides a chance for a rest while enjoying the view. Beyond, more climbing ensues, passing the track that branches off to Totara Flats Hut. Near Pig Flat, the three-sided Mountain House offers shelter and water. Beyond Mountain House, the track steepens for the final push up to Powell Hut. Now one of the most popular huts in Tararua Forest Park, Powell offers excellent views of the Wairarapa.

Powell Hut to Jumbo Hut (20 bunks, gas cookers, woodburner) 2.5–3.5 hours, 6.5 km

Above Powell Hut, a well-worn route leads up to Mt Holdsworth (1470 m), which is marked by a trig station. To reach Jumbo, drop down onto the ridge leading north in the direction indicated by a signpost. A well-worn trail leads across easy tussock tops, dropping steadily to a low saddle and then beginning a climb up past a tarn towards the peak. From Jumbo (1405 m), a signpost indicates the correct spur down to Jumbo Hut. Like Powell, Jumbo Hut offers extensive views eastwards.

Jumbo Hut to Atiwhakatu Hut (26 bunks, woodburner) 1.5 hours, 2.5 km

From Jumbo Hut, follow a steep but well-marked track down Raingauge Spur into the Atiwhakatu Valley, reaching the river just upstream of Atiwhakatu Hut.

Atiwhakatu Hut to Holdsworth Lodge 2–3 hours, 7 km

The track down the Atiwhakatu is well benched and bridged, providing all-weather access. It's fast travel to Holdsworth Creek, which is crossed by a swingbridge. Beyond, the track to Donnelly Flat passes some good viewpoints of the river's gorges. Donnelly Flat, with spots for camping, lies just 20 minutes from Holdsworth Lodge.

View of the tops and High Ridge from Mt Holdsworth

Grade Medium

Map Topo50 BP34 Masterton

Access Turn off State Highway 2 onto Norfolk Road 2 km south of Masterton. Follow Norfolk Road for 15 km to reach the end of Mt Holdsworth Road, where there is a large carpark, a camping area and toilets.

Huts All huts cost $15/night, or $7.50 for youths aged 11–17.

During the peak summer season (18 November to 30 April), Powell and Atiwhakatu huts must be booked in advance (www.doc.govt.nz). No booking is required for Jumbo Hut. Holdsworth Lodge is also available for overnight stays, but must be booked ahead.

Information DOC Whakaoriori/Masterton, 220 South Road, Masterton, tel: 06 377 0700, email: masterton@doc.govt.nz

REFERENCES AND FURTHER READING

Armitage, Don (ed.). *Great Barrier Island*, Canterbury University Press, Christchurch, 2001.

Barnett, Shaun. *North Island Weekend Tramps*, Craig Potton Publishing, Nelson, second edition 2008.

Barnett, Shaun and Rob Brown. *Classic Tramping in New Zealand*, Craig Potton Publishing, Nelson, second edition 2010.

Barnett, Shaun, Rob Brown and Geoff Spearpoint. *Shelter from the Storm: The story of New Zealand's backcountry huts*, Craig Potton Publishing, Nelson, 2012.

Barnett, Shaun and Chris Maclean. *Tramping: A New Zealand history*, Craig Potton Publishing, Nelson, 2014.

Beaglehole, Helen. *Lighting the Coast: A history of New Zealand's lighthouse system*, Canterbury University Press, Christchurch, 2006.

Beaglehole, Helen. *Always the Sound of the Sea: The daily lives of New Zealand lighthouse keepers,* Craig Potton Publishing, Nelson, 2009.

Bennett, Sarah and Lee Slater, *The New Zealand Tramper's Handbook*, Craig Potton Publishing, Nelson, 2010.

Brown, Rob. *Rakiura: The wilderness of Stewart Island,* Craig Potton Publishing, Nelson, 2006.

Chapple, Geoff. *A Walking Guide to New Zealand's Long Trail: Te Araroa*, Random House, Auckland, third edition 2014.

Dawson, John and Rob Lucas. *Nature Guide to the New Zealand Forest*, Godwit, Auckland, 2000.

Dawson, John and Rob Lucas. *Field Guide to New Zealand's Native Trees*, Craig Potton Publishing, Nelson, 2012.

Greenaway, Rob. *The Restless Land: Stories of Tongariro National Park*, DOC/Tongariro Natural History Society, Turangi, 1998.

Groves, Nick. *South Island Weekend Tramps,* Craig Potton Publishing, Nelson, second edition 2008.

Hegg, Danilo and Geoff Spearpoint (eds.) *Moir's Guide North: The Otago Southern Alps, from the Hollyford to Lake Ohau*, New Zealand Alpine Club, Christchurch, eighth edition, 2013.

Langton, Graham (ed.). *Mr Explorer Douglas: John Pascoe's New Zealand classic*, Canterbury University Press, Christchurch, 2000.

Leatham, Darrell. *The Golden Reefs: An account of the great days of quartz-mining at Reefton, Waiuta and the Lyell,* Nikau Press, Nelson, second edition 1994.

Maclean, Chris. *Tararua: The story of a mountain range,* Whitcombe Press, Wellington, 1994.

McNeill, Robin. *Moir's Guide South: The great southern lakes and fiords, south from the Hollyford*, eighth edition, 2008.

McNeill, Robin. *Safety in the Mountains*, Federated Mountain Clubs, Wellington, eleventh edition, 2012.

Mark, Alan F. *Above the Treeline: A nature guide to alpine New Zealand*, Craig Potton Publishing, Nelson, 2012.

Molloy, Les and Craig Potton. *New Zealand's Wilderness Heritage*, Craig Potton Publishing, Nelson, 2014.

Molloy, Les and Roger Smith. *Landforms: The shaping of New Zealand*, Craig Potton Publishing, Nelson, 2002.

Ombler, Kathy. *A Visitor's Guide to New Zealand National Parks,* New Holland, Auckland, 2005.

Pickering, Mark. *A Tramper's Journey*, Craig Potton Publishing, Nelson, 2004.

Pickering, Mark. *Huts: Untold stories of backcountry New Zealand*, Canterbury University Press, Christchurch, 2010.

Potton, Craig. *Great Walks of New Zealand*, Potton & Burton, Nelson, third edition, 2015.

Shaw, Derek. *Northwest Nelson Tramping Guide*, Nikau Press, Nelson, 1991.

Wilderness is a monthly magazine that regularly features articles on tramping, conservation, mountain biking, sea kayaking, climbing and natural history (see www.wildernessmag.com).

Tramper, Lagoon Saddle, Cass–Lagoon Saddle Track, Craigieburn Forest Park, Canterbury

EXPERIENCE MORE IN NEW ZEALAND'S OUTDOORS

Great Walks of New Zealand
CRAIG POTTON, WITH SHAUN BARNETT

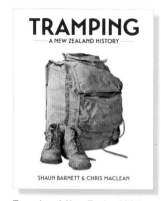

Tramping: A New Zealand history
SHAUN BARNETT & CHRIS MACLEAN

New Zealand Backcountry Cooking
PAUL & REBECCA GARLAND

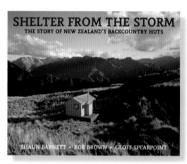

Shelter from the Storm: The story of
New Zealand's backcountry huts
SHAUN BARNETT, ROB BROWN
& GEOFF SPEARPOINT

Day Walks in New Zealand
SHAUN BARNETT & GEOGRAPHX

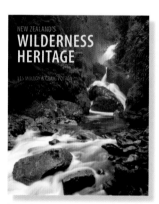

New Zealand's Wilderness Heritage
LES MOLLOY & CRAIG POTTON

Above the Treeline:
A nature guide to alpine
New Zealand
ALAN F MARK

Field Guide to New Zealand's
Native Trees
JOHN DAWSON & ROB LUCAS

Great Walks maps by
Geographx
- ABEL TASMAN TRACK
- HEAPHY TRACK
- KEPLER TRACK
- LAKE WAIKAREMOANA TRACK
- MILFORD TRACK
- RAKIURA TRACK
- ROUTEBURN TRACK
- TONGARIRO CIRCUIT
- WHANGANUI JOURNEY

PROUDLY BROUGHT TO YOU BY

pb potton & burton